A nostalgic look at

BELFAST

SLP

Silver Link Publishing Ltd

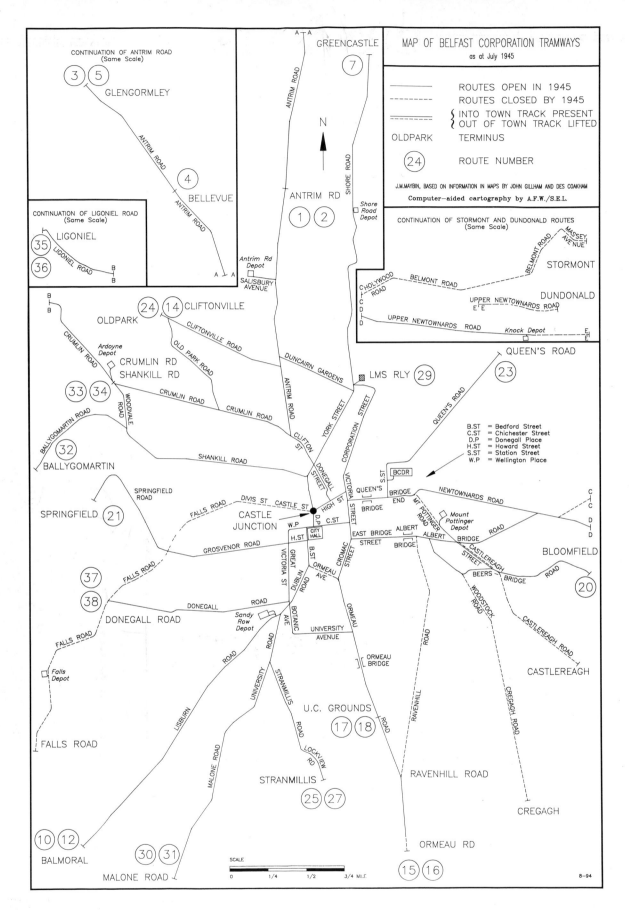

Map showing routes open at July 1945 (including access to Mountpottinger and Knock depots).
The only short workings shown are those listed in the public timetable and to which there was a regular service.

BELFAST TRAMS SINCE 1945

CONTENTS

McCreary 397, photographed in Donegall Square North in the early 1950s, leads a group of trams, including Chamberlain 382, heading towards Ligoniel and Crumlin Road. The (unchanged) destination blinds on the side of 397 read: 'BALMORAL / VIA GT VICTORIA ST / & CRUMLIN RD / & PASSES G N RY'. The three-line 'via' display was unusual.

The early type of 'Keep Left' sign and Belisha beacon mark the start of a tram traffic island. Potentially a major contribution to passenger safety, this practice was unfortunately not developed more widely in Belfast.

Alfred W. Mann's chemist shop at No 7 and Campbell's Patisserie, Cafe and Snackery at No 8 were replaced by the seven-storey Donegall House in 1968. Keen-eyed readers will observe the unusual lettering of 'Campbells' on the side of their building. Further up, the Athletic Stores building was replaced by the four-storey Sun Alliance House in 1985-6. *Photographer unknown*

© Mike Maybin 1994

Route maps
© J. C. Gillham and Des Coakham
General system map
© Stan Letts and Arthur Whitehouse

First published in November 1994

British Library Cataloguing in Publication Data

A catalogue record for this book is available from the British Library

ISBN 1 85794 030 X

Silver Link Publishing Ltd
Unit 5
Home Farm Close
Church Street
Wadenhoe
Peterborough PE8 5TE
Tel/fax (0832) 720440

Printed and bound in Great Britain

BELFAST TRAMS SINCE 1945

ACKNOWLEDGEMENTS

IN PREPARING this book I would like to acknowledge the help and support of many people, and while it is always difficult to select those to name and those to omit, I would particularly like to mention my wife Margaret and my children Andrew, James and Jenny. Although they know very little about Belfast trams - in spite of my influence - their contribution was in giving me the time and space to write the book. Without them it would never have been produced, although the house would have been painted and the cars would have been washed!

My thanks are due to David Harvey, who has written the companion volumes on Birmingham's trams in the series, for his introduction to Silver Link, for the use of a number of photographs from his collection, for reading a draft of the history and introduction sections and for his support and enthusiasm for the project.

My gratitude goes to Des Coakham and John Gillham, both for the use of their photographs and for allowing me to use their 1945 and 1938 track maps as the bases for the maps in the book.

To my long-time friends Cecil Slator and Richard Whitford my warmest thanks for their unstinting enthusiasm for all things connected with Belfast transport and specifically for access to their records, both photographic and written, which proved to be first-class sources of primary research material. They also read the introduction and history sections.

John Price not only gave permission to use several of his photographs but also offered to check the manuscript and, given his acknowledged expertise and his many other commitments, I am particularly grateful.

Roy Brook compiled one of the most comprehensive photographic records of Belfast trams in 1952 and 1953 and, not surprisingly, his is the largest single collection represented. I am grateful for his permission to draw so extensively on his work.

I would also like to acknowledge the information provided by Billy Montgomery, his son William and Michael Weir in relation to 'non-tram' vehicles in many of the photographs.

Central Belfast published by the Ulster Architectural Heritage Society in 1993 was an invaluable source of information on present-day buildings and in reminding me just how much central Belfast has changed in the last 40 years. I wish to acknowledge the use of their architectural descriptions on several occasions.

Finally, to all the people who agreed to the use of their photographs I offer my sincere appreciation. Where possible I have attributed each photograph to its copyright holder, but I apologise for any error or omission that may have occurred.

BIBLIOGRAPHY

Belfast Telegraph, *Bombs on Belfast* (1941)
Brett, C. E. B., *Buildings of Belfast, 1700-1914* (1985)
Hunter and Ludgate, *Gone But Not Forgotten* (1979)
Larmour, P., *Belfast - An Illustrated Architectural Guide* (1987)
Maguire, W. A., *Caught in Time* (1986)
Maybin, J. M., *Belfast Corporation Tramways* (1980)

Newham, A., *Cavehill & Whitewell Tramway* (Tramway Review Nos 61-63)
Open, M., *Fading Lights - Silver Screens* (1985)
PSV Circle, *NIRTB/UTA/Ulsterbus Fleet List* (1972)
    Belfast Corporation Fleet List (1968)
UAHS, *Central Belfast* (1993)
Walker and Dixon, *No Mean City* (1983)
    In Belfast Town (1984)

FOREWORD

John Cole

former Political Editor of the BBC

MY EARLIEST recollections of the Belfast trams, from the mid-'30s, were of their sound: the musical note of metal wheels on metal rails, its pitch rising as the tram gathered speed away from the stop at the top of our road. Our house was about 200 yards from the tram route along the Antrim Road. We lived in Skegoniel Avenue, which under its earlier name of Buttermilk Loney, or Lane, had been the terminus for the Antrim Road trams. But by my time these trams ran from the City Centre right out to Glengormley, then less the suburb that it is now than simply 'the end of the line'.

My father ran a small electrical contracting business, and was often called out late for emergency repair work at factories or houses. As a small boy I worried a lot when he was out late (with much less cause than small boys have in Belfast nowadays). So I used to listen in bed, from the time each tram drew away from the stop, hoping soon to hear his reassuring footsteps and the sound of his key in the door.

The nicest emergency work he had - certainly for my mother, brother and myself - was when the electrics at the Belfast Iceworks broke down. Then he would come down from the tram, much later than his usual teatime, but clutching a large carton of ice-cream that the manager had given him as a present for getting the Iceworks out of trouble. For most children, in the years before the war, ice-cream remained a luxury; it then disappeared during the war years. My most abiding memory of a wartime holiday in the Irish Free State, which was neutral, was of eating my first ice-cream in four or five years.

It was during the war that I started travelling on my own on the Belfast trams. I went to my grammar school, Belfast Royal Academy, the day after war broke out, and received my Senior Certificate (A Level equivalent) results on the day the first atomic bomb was dropped on Japan. The school was a couple of miles from my home, so when I was late or the weather was wet, I travelled by tram, rather than walking.

For children under 14 it cost a halfpenny (representing, over a week, a noticeable hole in most boys' pocket money). Those aged between 14 and 16 were still entitled to this minimum fare, provided that they had a Belfast Corporation Transport Department pass, confirming their ages and establishing that they were still at school.

The doyen of school-boy tram travellers on our stretch of line was a boy called 'Sticky' Reid. ('Sticky' was a kind of hereditary title, for it later passed to his brother. Years later, when my wife and I presented prizes to the West Country school where he was headmaster, I tantalised his pupils by references to his nickname, without finally revealing anything. The name derived from his infant penchant for lollipops, I believe.)

Right up to his final year at school, when he was pushing 18, 'Sticky' senior had contrived to hold on to his 'under 16' tram pass. Conductors were understandably incredulous, but could prove nothing. Possibly they admired his ingenuity. Anyhow, they contented themselves with heavy sarcasm. Did he have much trouble getting razor-blades (one of the wartime shortages)? 'Sticky' travelled on, unfazed.

Usually I went home for lunch - or dinner, as everybody then called it - but occasionally I joined some of the school-lunchers who had grown weary of the stolid fare provided, and travelled to the City Centre. Woolworth had just opened a cafeteria, a new and exotic concept, where there was not only delicious sausage-chips-and-baked-beans, but also iced water in a fountain, then also a novel luxury. The tram service was so reliable that we could be almost certain to get back in time for afternoon classes.

The Belfast trams suffered at least one blow in the Belfast air-raids. There was a tram depot about a quarter of a mile from where we lived, in Salisbury Avenue, and it received what must have been a direct hit in the Easter Tuesday raid of 1941. A thousand people, including two school friends of mine, who lived a couple of streets away, were killed - the worst death toll in a single night outside London and Coventry.

For schoolboys, many of the conductors developed as characters. One of them was learning French and German, and insisted on conducting conversations with those of us who confessed to taking classes in either or both of those languages. Another entertained us by singing. After I had left the school, which was on the top of a slope on the Cliftonville Road, my wife, then still a pupil there, saw a tram that careered down to the Antrim Road and buried itself in the front of the Phoenix pub. Nobody was seriously hurt, and the Phoenix soon rose from its ashes.

Most of the Belfast trams in my time were blue, but the original models, called, I believe, 'Standard Reds', were popular with the young, because they not only had open platforms downstairs, but open areas at the back and front of the top deck, from which you could shout at friends, or, indeed, enemies.

They were also popular with two other groups, football supporters and shipyard workers. In each case those trams carried far more than their prescribed number of passengers, because both the fans, who were anxious to get to a match, and the workers coming home from the Harland & Wolff shipyard, were happy to stand illegally on every open space, and even hang on around the fender at the back. Only rarely did a conductor try to enforce the regulations: no standing on the platform or top deck.

However, a zealous conductor once sternly informed the illegal standers and hangers-on that his tram would not move another inch until those areas had been cleared. To underline his determination, he himself stepped down on to the road. This proved to be a mistake. A knowing traveller at once gave a double chug on the bell. The driver was not able to see his conductor, stranded on the road, so assuming that he had given the signal, drove off. The conductor was left to catch up by taking a lift on the next one. This was taken generally in Belfast tramcar mythology to be proof of the saying that the customer - or passenger as we called him/her in those days - was always right.

Public transport in Belfast has suffered terribly during the present troubles. At one point bus-burning was usually among the first moves by those starting a riot. This was not the first time that things like that have happened. My mother used to tell me stories of the period of civil unrest in the early 1920s. She was then working in the City Centre, and travelled by tram to and from her parents' home in Greencastle, then a village along the shore of Belfast Lough. The route ran through a politically 'mixed' area, York Street. On turbulent days conductors advised their passengers to lie on the floor of the tram as they passed streets from which gunmen had been known to take a casual pot-shot at passing trams.

A happier memory from the same period: my mother-in-law, whose family lived several miles past Glengormley, used to cycle to and from that terminus, leaving her bicycle there (doubtless without a chain, in those more honest times). But like most country people she was sensitive to superstitions from the natural world: if she saw two magpies on her ride to the tram, all would be well. But if she saw one, she would expect to find, when she alighted from the tram that evening to ride home, that a slow puncture had left her with a flat tyre to repair.

INTRODUCTION

BELFAST trams have not received as much as attention as some other mainland systems in the sense that no one has yet written the definitive history. Only two books have been produced on Belfast Trams. The first, *Gone but not Forgotten*, was published in 1979 jointly by the Irish Transport Trust and the Railway Preservation Society of Ireland. It was primarily a collection of photographs, while my own *Belfast Corporation Tramways 1905-54* is essentially a reprint of a series of articles that first appeared in *Tramway Review* some years earlier. Although illustrated, it is mainly a history of the system written from the perspective of a tram enthusiast. Both volumes have been out of print for many years.

This book attempts to combine an increasing interest in local history with an increasing awareness of the value of rail-borne urban public transport. As its title suggests it is primarily a photographic record, with extended captions, of Belfast trams between 1945 and the end of the system in February 1954. However, there is a small number of photographs outside this period.

The layout of the photographs is on a route-by-route basis, starting with the City Centre and working roughly clockwise from Queen's Road to Greencastle. This is followed by depot views and finally two views of ex-horse car 249 and Chamberlain 357, which are thankfully preserved.

By 1945 several routes no longer had trams running on them. Falls Road and most of the East Belfast tram routes had been converted to trolleybus operation. The Ravenhill Road route - never very profitable - became bus-operated from 1940 with a reduced service. Ormeau Road via Botanic Avenue had been prematurely converted to bus operation in 1945 because of major roadworks. Bloomfield followed in 1946, Cliftonville Road and Donegall Road in 1947, and Ormeau Road via Cromac Street in 1948. Bloomfield was converted to trolleybuses, Cliftonville Road and Donegall Road to motor buses and Ormeau via Cromac Street to trolleybuses. However, Cliftonville Road was converted again in 1951 - this time to trolleybuses! There is, therefore, rather an imbalance of photographs available for certain routes for the early post-war period, and inevitably this is reflected, to some extent, in the selection of photographs in the book.

In many ways Belfast followed traditional British practice in its tramways. For example, all the cars were four-wheeled double-deckers. Electric current was collected from an overhead wire via a trolley pole that had to be turned at the terminus. Trams were double-ended and 'reversed' at stub crossovers in the track. All track was double with the exception of the portion between Bellevue and Glengormley.

My own memory of Belfast trams is limited to their last few years of operation in the 1950s, when as a child we visited my grandmother and travelled by trolleybus from the Ormeau Road to the City Centre, then by tram to Bray Street on the Crumlin Road. By then it was left to the more modern Moffetts, Chamberlains and McCrearys to provide the backbone of the service, and I never had the pleasure of riding on one of the old Standard Reds.

I have other memories of riding the Crumlin Road cars in the rush-hour, full of shipyard men in damp coats, the ringing of the bell to stop or start, the good-humoured banter of the conductors, the careful counting out of pennies and halfpennies to make up the correct fare, and the occasional dispute about a youth's age and therefore his right to travel half-fare.

Apart from the McCreary cars, Belfast trams had no platform doors. On the platform beside the motorman there was a leather-covered chain designed to deter passengers from getting on or off, and the strict rule was that the chain should be kept across at all times. On one occasion on a cold and windy day a tram was passing Castle Junction with the chain not in place. It was stopped by the duty Inspector and the motorman loudly told in front of all the passengers to 'put that—chain on'. Quick as a flash the motorman replied, equally loudly, 'Thanks, Billy, I wondered where the draught was coming from'!

In the early days of trams, fares were a penny and twopence and conductors were required to carry a certain amount of change for a shilling, or occasionally, a half-crown. There was a gentleman who lived on the Malone Road route who got into the habit of offering a 10-shilling note for his penny fare into town in the morning. Remembering that 10 shillings might be a week's wages for a working man, few conductors could change this amount first thing in the morning. There was no choice but to allow him to travel free. One conductor, becoming fed up with this behaviour, decided to deal with the matter in his own way. The next time he was faced with the 'Sorry I've only got a 10-bob note', he replied 'No problem, sir, I've got some change this morning', and handed the passenger 119 penny coins. He did not have any more trouble from that particular gentleman!

Although working on the trams was considered relatively secure employment, especially at a time when casual labour was widespread, conductors and drivers were not particularly well paid. Tickets came in packs and were held by elastic bands in a rack carried by the conductor. As the serial numbers were recorded on issue at the depot in the morning and again at pay-in in the evening, the cash due was easily calculated. On occasions, when short of money, conductors would sell tickets from the middle of the rack, where the loss was not immediately noticed. However, the money had to be found by the time the tickets had been sold as far down as the 'gap'. The practice could result in disciplinary action, but was often regarded as 'borrowing' rather than theft, and was referred to by the crews as 'selling on the futures market'.

Although this book is primarily about trams, it is also a

commentary about how Belfast has changed in the last 40 years. While Belfast, like most cities, has suffered from poor planning decisions, it has also borne the brunt of many terrorist car-bombs, resulting, among other things, in the loss of a number of fine buildings. I have included a number of 'before and after' photographs that show both some of the changes that have taken place and, in a few cases, a remarkable continuity.

Viewed from the uncertainties of the 1990s, the '50s appear stable, solid and secure. Public transport was reliable, predictable and frequent. It was clean, cheap and comfortable and the staff were knowledgeable, helpful and courteous. The weather, of course, was better too!

There were several ways in which Belfast trams were unusual as compared to other cities. Belfast conductors wore their ticket machines and cash bags around the same shoulder - usually the right - whereas in most other places they were worn on opposite shoulders with the straps crossing across the chest. By 1945 tram routes that crossed the City Centre showed a different route number in each direction, which was changed at the terminus. It was partly for this reason that Belfast people almost always defined routes by their name and not the number. The other reason was that many of the Standard Reds never carried route numbers.

There were a couple of other things of which I was aware; I don't know whether they were unique or just unusual. Boys selling the local evening paper - the *Belfast Telegraph* - were allowed to travel free while so engaged. According to the rule book newspapers were the only item allowed to be sold on the trams. Old people from Nazareth Lodge on the Ravenhill Road were allowed to travel up and down on the trams and buses free outside the rush-hour. I remember this particularly

as it was the first time I had seen a man smoking a pipe with what seemed to be a metal lid. I must have been about eight at the time.

I was delighted when John Cole agreed to write the Foreword to this book. He was born in Belfast in 1927, lived for a major portion of his boyhood in Skegoniel Avenue off the Antrim Road, and went to school at the nearby Belfast Royal Academy. He joined the *Belfast Telegraph* as a reporter in 1945, and from then until 1956 was by turns industrial, municipal and finally political correspondent. He left Belfast for the (then) *Manchester Guardian* working as reporter, labour correspondent, news editor and deputy editor. From there he moved to a similar post with the *Observer* where he remained from 1975 to 1981. In that year he was appointed Political Editor of the BBC - an extremely high-profile post - and the one for which he will probably be best remembered. He is a graduate of London University and has received honorary doctorates from Queen's, Belfast, Ulster, St Andrew's and the Open University.

He retired in 1992 and is currently writing a book of political memoirs that is due for publication in 1995. During his 'retirement' he has contributed a twice weekly slot on BBC's 'Westminster Live'; works on BBC1's 'On the Record' and has appeared on several 'Holiday' programmes. On the occasion of his retirement John Major described him as 'a national institution'. The late Labour leader John Smith referred to his 'integrity and political perception', while Paddy Ashdown described him as 'dedicated, sharp and observant'.

Years ago my uncle gave me a coin upon which were inscribed the words 'In Memory of the Good Old Days'. It was dated 1794! As the following pages will show, I am an unashamed lover of reminiscing.

A BRIEF HISTORY OF BELFAST TRAMWAYS

BEFORE 1872 public transport in Belfast was provided mainly by a small network of horse bus services. In August of that year the Belfast Street Tramways Company (BST) opened the first horse tramcar route, which operated from Castle Place to Botanic Gardens by way of Donegall Place, Wellington Place, Great Victoria Street and University Road.

In February 1873 a second line was built from Albert Memorial via Victoria Street, Corporation Street, Great George's Street and York Street to the magnificent terminus of the Belfast & Northern Counties Railway (BNCR). Regrettably this building was badly damaged in the Blitz of 1941, and although partially restored after the war, was eventually demolished in 1977.

At the start five cars operated a 9-minute frequency to

Botanic Gardens and a 15-minute service to the BNCR station, but in the early days passengers had to walk between the Albert Memorial and Castle Place. The service, which was initially very successful, used one-horse single-deck cars, and the Company charged a universal fare of twopence irrespective of the distance travelled.

The original Act specified mostly single line with passing loops at the standard Irish Railway gauge of 5 ft 3 in. It was hoped that this would allow through traffic from the railway to use the tram track, although of course the wheel profile of railway carriages would have required a tramway gauge of 5 ft 2¼ in. This connection was not built, but the BST later laid a siding into the station, which provided a very welcome undercover transfer between tram and train.

By 1876 three new lines had been added to the system. An additional route connected Castle Place to the BNCR by way of Bridge Street, Lower Donegall Street and York Street, while lines were also constructed to Agincourt Avenue on the Ormeau Road and Richmond on the Antrim Road.

In 1878 the BST obtained an Act that, besides authorising certain extensions, allowed the Company to change the track gauge to the British Standard of 4 ft 8½ in. The reason for doing this has never been entirely clear. However, in the event the gauge as constructed was 4 ft 9 in, and this was carried right through to the end of tramcars in 1954.

By 1881 the Manager, a Mr Totten, had developed rather an odd route pattern. The six routes that operated were:

1 Richmond to Botanic Gardens by way of Antrim Road, Clifton Street, Donegall Street, Bridge Street, High Street, Castle Place, Donegall Place, Wellington Place, Great Victoria Street and University Road.

2 BNCR station to Windsor (Lisburn Road) by way of York Street, Great George's Street, Corporation Street, High Street, Castle Place, then as route 1 as far as Bradbury Place, then Lisburn Road to Windsor.

3 BNCR station to the corner of York Street and Donegall Street.

4 Albert Memorial to Connswater via Victoria Street, Queen's Bridge, Bridge End, Mountpottinger Road, Albertbridge Road and Newtownards Road to Connswater Bridge.

5 Corn Market to Ormeau Bridge by way of High Street, Victoria Street, Cromac Street and Ormeau Road.

6 Castle Place to Crumlin Road via Bridge Street, Donegall Street, Clifton Street and Crumlin Road to the County Courthouse.

However, within a few years the Company's financial problems were giving sufficient concern to persuade the London directors to investigate the Belfast operation. Among their findings were poor track and car maintenance, bad time-keeping and an illogical route pattern that did not meet the needs of the passengers and made transfer between cars difficult and time-wasting. Further areas for concern were poor health in the horse stud and a generally inefficient use of resources, which resulted in unnecessarily high expenditure when compared to the service offered.

Besides holding a seat on the Belfast Board, the investigating officer was a director of a number of tramway companies on the mainland. He was horrified at the state of the Company and immediately replaced Totten by a young civil engineer from Portsmouth called Andrew Nance, who was given the task of turning the Company round.

Nance took up the post in November 1881, but within a couple of days came to the conclusion that his task was hopeless. There is a story, probably apocryphal, that he went to pray in St George's Church. It is said that he saw a vision from which he received inspiration and went on to tackle the job of reorganising the tramways. True or not,

Nance chose to remain with Belfast Tramways for the best part of 35 years.

In 1884 the old Hercules Street was swept away and replaced by Royal Avenue in the first major city centre redevelopment scheme. Strict parameters were enforced for the construction of new buildings, which resulted in their being of similar height, frontal design, ornamentation and quality of construction. Although regrettable planning decisions and terrorist bombs have dented the essential 'unity' of the Avenue, sufficient of it remains intact, particularly above ground floor level, to show clearly the original intention.

Following the opening of Royal Avenue, the tramway company transferred five of its six routes from Bridge Street to the new thoroughfare in 1885. This decision confirmed the importance of the development and caused understandable concern to the traders in Donegall Street and Bridge Street. Nance arranged the routes and services in such a way that most parts of the system offered a 5-minute frequency, apart from the Crumlin and Ormeau Road routes which were 10 minutes. However, from York Street to Bradbury Place cars operated every 2½ minutes in each direction. He also timed departures to give good connections in the City Centre.

With the opening of Royal Avenue the term 'Castle Junction' was born. Although this phrase is as familiar to Belfast people as Sauchiehall Street is to Glaswegians, it appears on no street sign, nor does it form part of any address. It is purely a tramway term, although used as often today as when the trams stopped running 40 years ago. For very many years almost all services passed 'The Junction' and young children were told that if they got lost in Belfast they were to get on a tram and stay there as it would eventually come to Castle Junction. They were then to get off and present themselves to the Inspector on duty who would put them on the right tram home!

The following ten years saw the Belfast Street Tramways Company prosper and expand. In 1885 it owned 61 trams and 470 horses, and carried 5.8 million passengers over about 12 miles of track. By 1895 the company owned 104 cars and 920 horses, and carried about 11 million passengers over about 24 miles of track. Andrew Nance set a pattern of management and operation that was to last until his retirement in 1916, and many of his policies and practices lasted until the end of tramway operation.

Residents in the Bellevue and Glengormley areas were keen to have 'tramway accommodation', as they called it, and tried to persuade the BST to build a line. As the Company was busy expanding in other directions, it felt that its resources were already sufficiently stretched, and declined. Nance also had reservations about the financial viability of a line serving a relatively thinly populated area. Eventually a group of local businessmen got together to form the Cavehill & Whitewell Tramway Company (C&W) to build a route from the BST terminus at Chichester Park on the Antrim Road to Glengormley village. The line was opened for business on Saturday 1 July 1882 with a small steam engine (believed to be a Kitson 0-4-0 with roof condensers) pulling passenger trailers, though at various times horses were used as well. This line was owned and operated completely independently of the BST.

The initial agreement between Belfast Corporation and the Belfast Street Tramways Company was for 21 years, after which the local authority would have the right of purchase. Extensive but generally amicable negotiations took place, and before the deadline (August 1893) a settlement had been reached. In return for agreeing not to exercise its powers of compulsory purchase for a further 14 years (ie until 1907), Belfast Corporation would receive £4,000 per annum rental for the first seven years and £5,000 per year for the remaining seven.

At around this time experiments in mechanical traction were taking place, and Belfast Corporation was anxious not to be left behind. In 1894 a scheme was drawn up based on cable haulage, but did not progress beyond the talking stage. From 1896 Belfast's arch-rival, Dublin, installed electric traction on its routes and pressure became intense on the Belfast Corporation and BST to electrify and expand their system.

While the questions of purchase and electrification were being discussed, considerable pressure built up for expansion of the service to certain districts. The Company did not wish to finance this work itself - at least until its future tenure was settled. Separate companies were therefore set up to build routes to Ligoniel, Sydenham (Strandtown) and into the Belfast & County Down Railway (BCDR) station. These companies raised the capital and laid the track, which they then leased back to the BST, which owned and operated the cars and retained the fare receipts. The companies were operated integrally with the rest of the system until the BST bought the Ligoniel and Sydenham undertakings in 1903. The BCDR line was also worked by the BST until purchased by the Belfast Corporation in 1905.

However, while the two sides had no problem in agreeing that expansion and electrification were highly desirable in principle, they were unable to agree upon the terms. Essentially the Company wished to secure as long a lease as possible to justify the necessary capital expenditure, while the Corporation wished to buy the system and convert it to electric traction as soon as possible. In 1896 the BST drafted a Bill that would have allowed it to build electric tramways to Holywood, Newtownards, Comber, Carrickfergus and Lisburn. This was part of a ploy to force the Corporation to extend the Company's lease by encouraging popular dissent at the comparison between what would have become the old slow Corporation horse trams and the fast modern Company electric cars.

These proposals, though developed to the point of detailed costings, were not put into operation, and as a stop-gap measure, the Corporation built a number of lines itself. The lines to Malone, Stranmillis, Knock, Ravenhill Road, Cliftonville and Springfield Road were authorised by the Belfast Corporation Act of 1899 and opened for traffic in 1900. As with Ligoniel and Sydenham, the Company owned the cars and horses, retained the receipts, paid a rental to the Corporation and operated the routes integrally with the remainder of the network.

The disagreement was eventually resolved by the Belfast Corporation (Tramways) Act 1904, which allowed the Corporation compulsorily to buy the BST together with the tiny tramway owned by the Belfast & County Down Railway. The price, decided by arbitration, was £356,948 14s 6d. Besides authorising extensions to Greencastle, Ligoniel, Dundonald, Queen's Road, Cliftonville Road, Woodvale Road, and link lines in Castle Street and Duncairn Gardens, the Act allowed the Corporation to electrify the entire system.

Vesting day was 1 January 1905, and on 19 January the main contracts were let to J. G. White of London. Considerable work was involved in the change. The jobs of erecting the overhead wires, laying the underground cables, building a major expansion to the generating station and laying the track were the responsibility of the contractors and supervised by other Corporation departments. Nance was responsible for the purchase of 170 electric cars, and the conversion of 50 horse cars and five depots to electric traction. He was also involved in the construction of one entirely new depot (Shore Road), and at the same time was expected to maintain an efficient horse car network! It was intended to complete all this work by 1 September 1905. However, this time-scale proved to be optimistic and it was 5 December before the Belfast City Tramways (BCT) system was fully operational. Nevertheless, the conversion in Belfast was still one of the fastest in the United Kingdom. With the exceptions of two small interlaced sections in Castle Street and Great Edward (now Victoria) Street, all the routes were constructed as double track. Victoria Street was widened and 'double tracked' in the late 1920s.

Nance had been manager with the BST for 24 years when the Corporation assumed control. By this time he had acquired a great deal of experience of the travel patterns of Belfast people, which he put to good use in the design of the route network and fares structure of the new electric tramways. Essentially he used a system of multiple destinations where each terminus was linked to several others through the city centre. For example, Balmoral was linked with Antrim Road via Carlisle Circus, the BNCR station via York Street, Knock via Queen's Bridge and Knock via Albert Bridge. Each of these services operated at 20-minute intervals, giving a combined frequency of 5 minutes between Balmoral and the City Centre.

Because of the multiple destinations, Nance argued that with care and forward planning a passenger could get a car from one terminus to almost any other. With 14 routes radiating from Castle Junction like spokes of a wheel, and a choice of between two and six destinations from each, he exaggerated somewhat. The system of fares established by Nance was one penny per mile from Castle Junction 'as the crow flies', with a maximum of twopence on each car.

The main pressures on Nance at this time were fares, routes and staff. In company days he had reported to the Board in London and had enjoyed almost complete autonomy in Belfast. Under local authority control, policy rested with the Tramways Committee who were susceptible to local political pressure and sometimes sought to exercise day-to-day management. The main areas of contention were staff, routes and fares and stages. Nance did not easily take to the detailed supervision and control that some councillors wished to exert, and resented what he perceived to be interference. Nance was clear that the system of fares and stages established in 1905 should not be changed, and apart from one or two unsuccessful and short-lived experiments, no changes took place until after his retirement in 1916.

Shortly after electrification the General Manager introduced a rule book that was required to be carried by every employee. It was beautifully produced with red leather covers and gold edging to the leaves. Some of the rules would be difficult to enforce in today's equal opportunity culture: General Rule 8 stated that 'MOTORMEN and CONDUCTORS are expected to live as near as possible to the relief point of the Depot to which they are attached'. In Belfast General Rule 23 was an absolute necessity! 'MOTORMEN and CONDUCTORS while in uniform must not wear any flower, emblem or decoration of any kind. They are expected to refrain from taking any active part in any Municipal or General Elections whether on or off duty. If they are discovered doing so WHILE ON DUTY, they will certainly be dismissed.'

The Queen's Road route was not opened until 1908. Although worked integrally with the Corporation's system, the tramway was on land controlled by Belfast Harbour Commissioners (BHC) and it remained in that ownership until closure in 1954. An interesting sidelight was the BHC's insistence on having its own monogram on the traction poles! One rather unusual feature of this route was that, near the Abercorn basin, a section of the overhead could be raised to allow abnormal loads like ships' propellers and boilers to pass. Another interesting aspect was that the overhead was supported on centre poles right until the end of tramway operation.

Also in 1908 the Corporation built a neat little wooden hexagonal hut with a tiled roof at Castle Junction in which the duty Inspector worked. Although only a handful of people could squeeze inside, it provided public information, acted as a lost property office and generally dealt with minor operational problems. It quickly became known as the 'Tramwaymen's Dance Hall'.

In 1909, in response to pressure from local politicians, Nance produced a report on possible expansion of the system and recommended routes to Donegall Road, Castlereagh, Bloomfield, Botanic Avenue, Oldpark, Holywood and McArt's Fort near Cavehill. He also recommended extensions to Ligoniel, Stranmillis and the purchase of the Cavehill & Whitewell Tramway Company, which he described as 'the only Tramway under alien control within 60 miles of the City of Belfast'. He was very keen on the line to McArt's Fort, stating: 'I venture to make the proposition that this immense boon [Cavehill] given to Belfast by Nature, shall by the agency of the Tramway Committee, be made accessible to the feeblest and oldest citizen for the small payment of 3d.' Regretfully the rather more prosaic committee declined to build this line or the one to Holywood. However, the other lines were built and opened for business on 28 January 1913.

True to form, Nance chose to link Oldpark with Castlereagh via Queen's Bridge, and Donegall Road with Bloomfield via Albert Bridge; this had the merit of not disrupting the existing route pattern. The Botanic Avenue route replaced Ormeau Avenue, which had been unremunerative for some years.

The Cavehill & Whitewell was absorbed by the Corporation under the Belfast Corporation Act of 1910 and vested on 1 June 1911. The following day, Corporation cars ran right through to Glengormley, although for some months before, Corporation tickets bore the following inscription on the obverse: 'The Glengormley Tramway is now worked by the Corporation; the cars run from the City Hall, and there is now no change of car. Cheap fares, beau-

tiful scenery, tea house and other attractions at the end of the line. Look out for the opening of the NEW Bellevue Gardens.'

This was a reference to about 32 acres of land at Drumnadrough, which the C&W owned and upon which was situated its headquarters and depot. As the BCT had its own depot at Salisbury Avenue, Nance hoped to develop the area into a huge natural playground. He constructed a plateau part way up the hill, which was made accessible by a series of gentle zigzag paths and a magnificent floral staircase; although it is no longer in use, the staircase is still there. A tea house was constructed, and the area was widely promoted by the Tramways Department as an ideal spot for a family day out.

Unfortunately serious subsidence took place that caused bulging of the boundary walls, slipping of the slopes and ultimately fracturing of the concrete staircase. The tea house was burned down by suffragettes in 1914, and in view of the political uncertainty that led to the First World War, development work was suspended.

In 1916, aged 69, Nance retired, having served Belfast Tramways for 35 years. Though not universally popular, judging by the contemporary comments in Robert McElborough's *The Autobiography of a Working Man*, he was held in some considerable respect by his men. It is perhaps some measure of the professional regard in which he was held by the Corporation that he was awarded a consultancy at £500 per year (about one-third of his salary). To many, Nance personified Belfast Tramways - he certainly had a profound effect on their development.

He was succeeded by James S. D. Moffett, General Manager of West Ham Corporation Tramways, and like Nance he was a civil engineer. Passenger traffic continued to grow: in 1905 the trams carried about 30 million passengers, and by 1916 the figure had more than doubled to 64 million, while the number of cars had increased from 170 to 290. The period was characterised by justifiable complaints of overcrowding, and Moffett obtained permission to buy 50 new trams of a totally enclosed design. These were known as the 'Moffett' cars from the start, and the tradition grew up of naming new trams after the General Manager of the time. They were built by the Brush Electrical Company of Loughborough and seated 68 people - an increase of 12 over the 'Standard Reds', as the original cars became known. Other new features of these cars were a near-side front exit for quicker boarding and alighting at Castle Junction, a larger wheelbase truck, more powerful motors and platform vestibules for the protection of motormen.

The cars were a great success and were seen as forerunners of a modern fleet of which Belfast might be proud. Although ridership had greatly increased, so had costs at an even greater rate, and the Tramways Committee urgently sought ways of economising. One of the obvious ways it chose was to reduce the frequency of service at off-peak times.

Although acutely aware of the need to economise, the Committee came under pressure to build more extensions. During the immediate post-war years it considered where best to do so, and the Belfast Corporation Acts of 1923 and 1924 authorised the following works:

1 An extension of the Belmont line from Massey Avenue

junction to the gates of Stormont - the seat of the Northern Ireland Parliament. (However, the line was built long before Parliament Building was completed, and for a period the only tram service along the extension was a few workmen's cars in the morning and evening.)

2 An extension of the Knock line from the City Boundary to the gates of Dundonald cemetery.

3 A link line joining Donegall Square North to Victoria Street along Chichester Street.

4 A line along Ballygomartin Road from Woodvale Road to Forth River bridge.

Besides these, several curves and crossovers were laid in to facilitate special traffic movements. One notable movement, which caused traffic chaos in later years, was that from Ann Street to Victoria Street. There was no problem with cars coming from the Shipyard and turning left into Victoria Street; however, cars going in the other direction came up Victoria Street on the left, crossed over to the opposite tracks on the right-hand side of the road and turned right. They then crossed to the left-hand track in Ann Street, much to the consternation of drivers coming in the opposite direction! (This was one of the few places in Belfast where a points boy could still be seen.) All these lines were opened by 1925, and although it was not realised at the time, these were to be the last significant route extensions in Belfast.

The early 1920s saw two major developments in Belfast. The first was the rise of terrorism, which surrounded the establishment of the state of Northern Ireland and the Irish Free State. There was a number of attacks on the tramcars and on depots, and for a period some cars ran with wire netting over the windows to protect passengers from missiles. John Cole refers to this in his Foreword.

Partly because of 'The Troubles', in July 1922 Moffett applied for and was offered the General Managership of Salford Corporation Transport. He was succeeded in Belfast by Samuel Carlisle - the first local man to hold the post. Although without formal academic or professional qualifications, Carlisle's experience with the BST and BCT since 1899 was considered to be more important.

The other significant phenomenon was the rise in private bus operators. A change in legislation transferred the licensing of privately owned buses from the Belfast Corporation to the newly formed Ministry of Home Affairs. It also enabled the local authority to frame bye-laws to protect its tramways.

For whatever reason, Belfast Corporation did not get around to considering new bye-laws. Carlisle warned the Tramways Committee on several occasions of the consequences of failing to do so, but he was not heeded. In the spring of 1928 the private bus owners realised that they now had 'free rein' to operate in Belfast, and in June began to compete vigorously with the trams. Not only did this adversely affect Corporation revenues, but safety was also compromised as buses raced trams to pick up passengers.

Private bus owners were not slow to provide services where trams did not operate; good examples of such routes were Cherryvalley and Downview Avenue. The situation developed to the point of chaos with bus services opening and closing as operators searched for the most lucrative routes. By the early autumn the operators had formed a loose combination - the Ulster Motor Coach Owners Association - and both sides began to appreciate that the current chaotic and unrestrained situation could not continue. They opened negotiations and reached an agreement whereby the Belfast Corporation was given the monopoly of operating within its area, and in return the local authority undertook to continue to operate a number of bus routes, bought 50 buses from the private operators and employed a number of their drivers.

The Corporation was seriously embarrassed by this debacle and needed a scapegoat. Carlisle was chosen and, although he retained his salary, was demoted to Deputy General Manager. The main job was advertised and William Chamberlain of Leeds was appointed. Taking up the post in November 1928, his first task was to update the ageing tramcar fleet, and he ordered the rebuilding of 50 of the best Standard Reds. Chamberlain's modernisation programme included a new totally enclosed body, and upholstered seats on both decks with garden seats instead of longitudinal ones downstairs. The cars were painted blue, and this came to be the recognised sign of modern trams in Belfast. Some were fitted for a period with 50 hp motors. The first car to enter service was 164, and was photographed at Stranmillis in February 1929 (see page 57).

He also ordered 50 new cars, of which 40 were built by the Brush Electrical Company of Loughborough and ten by the Service Motor Works of Belfast. The new cars had two 50 hp motors and, like the Moffetts, seated 68. They were also provided with electric heaters, upholstered seats and air brakes. As they were the first air-braked cars in Belfast, warning triangles were placed at the ends to warn unsuspecting motorists. The new batch of cars began to arrive in 1930, and quickly acquired the name 'Chamberlains'. They were allocated fleet numbers 342-391.

Also at about this time Chamberlain arranged to recondition the 50 Moffett cars by installing high-speed motors. However, it was some time before all the batch received upholstered seats and air brakes. As the trams were reconditioned they were repainted blue.

Chamberlain continued to operate a protectionist fares policy in favour of the tramcars, notwithstanding that the municipality now enjoyed monopoly status as providers of public passenger transport in the City. In 1931 Chamberlain left Belfast to take up the post of Chairman of the North Western Traffic Commissioners and was succeeded by Robert McCreary.

McCreary was a distinguished professional engineer, having obtained a first class BSc in 1912. He worked briefly in the City Surveyor's Department of Belfast Corporation before war service; he was awarded the MC in 1916. On returning to Belfast with the rank of Major, he became Permanent Way Engineer with the Tramways Department, overseeing the 1922-5 route extensions and the major track renewals of the early '20s.

The early 1930s were some of the most stable years in the department's history. The number of tramcars operated, the numbers of passengers carried, tramcar mileage and income all showed a gentle year-on-year increase. Although similar trends were evident in the bus operation, the latter vehicles provided less than 10 per cent of the total service. For most of the 1930s the motorbuses were restricted to a supporting role.

Aware of the unfavourable comparisons sometimes made between 30-year-old trams and two-year-old buses in terms of comfort and speed, McCreary embarked upon a modernisation programme for trams and, in what had now become rather a Belfast tradition, ordered 50 new cars. The first two appeared in service in April 1935; 20 were constructed by the English Electric Company, the remainder being built by Service Motor Works. The 'McCreary' cars, as they inevitably became known, were of a streamlined design with upholstered seats, improved staircase access and, for the first time, stop lights and, in the English Electric cars, direction arrows. In addition the cars were liberally equipped with destination and route blinds. As delivered, the McCrearys were vaguely reminiscent of the Blackpool 'Balloon' cars, which still operate on the Promenade route. Unlike those of Blackpool, however, the Belfast cars were all four-wheelers.

At this time on the British mainland serious consideration was being given to trolleybuses, and inevitably Belfast turned its attention in that direction. In 1936 permission was sought and obtained for a trial trolleybus route, and on 28 March 1938 trolleybuses replaced tramcars on the Falls Road route. As the experiment was an unqualified success, the Corporation agreed in 1939 to abandon tramcars in favour of trolleybuses throughout the City.

In September 1940 the Ravenhill tramway route was converted to bus operation with a reduced frequency - mainly because passenger levels were not thought sufficiently high to justify the capital expenditure of installing trolleybus overhead.

Although the Second World War slowed down the delivery of the new trolleybuses and overhead equipment, Cregagh was converted on 13 February 1941, Castlereagh on 5 June the same year, and Stormont on 26 March 1942. Dundonald via Queen's Bridge saw its last trams on 15 November, while the Albert Bridge leg of the route lasted until 7 March 1943. This was to be the last conversion of the war.

Although the tramcar route mileage had been significantly reduced, the number of passengers carried continued to increase. In response to this, as cars were released from routes converted to trolleybus operation, they were transferred to the remaining tram routes.

Almost all East Belfast services were operated by trolleybuses by early 1945. The main exception was Queen's Road, which still required a large number of tramcars. In the rush-hour this route was busier even than the famous Embankment service in London, and a nose-to-tail procession of cars snaked out of Station Street and over Queen's Bridge every evening. Many shipyard workers rode (quite illegally) on the fenders, not only to get home quickly, but also because there was a good chance of the conductor being unable to collect all the fares.

One interesting operation after the war was getting to and from Mountpottinger depot. With the abandonment of the track between Bridge End and the depot in 1937, trams going into the depot thereafter used Albert Bridge and turned right into Castlereagh Street, where the conductor turned the trolley. The tram then reversed over the crossover, crossed back over the junction of Albertbridge Road with Castlereagh Street, went down Mountpottinger Road, then turned right into the depot. The reverse procedure was a bit simpler in that cars turned left out of the depot into Mountpottinger Road, left again into Albertbridge Road, left again at the Ropeworks Junction, down the Newtownards Road and over the Queen's Bridge. The curve from Albertbridge Road into Newtownards Road was the last piece of new tramway track laid in Belfast.

During the immediate post-war years in Belfast a number of developments took place in quick succession. The policy of replacing trams by trolleybuses continued. Although the Ormeau route via Botanic Avenue was temporarily replaced by buses on 14 January 1945 because of major sewer works, this became permanent. Bloomfield closed on 5 May 1946 and Cliftonville on 31 August 1947. On 19 April 1948 the service to Ormeau via Cromac Street was replaced by trolleybuses, and on 24 January 1949 the longest route on the system, Glengormley, operated tramcars for the last time.

Colonel McCreary, as he had become after further distinguished service in the Second World War, which included the laying of light railways, retired in 1951 and was replaced by Joseph Mackle. Mackle's background was primarily motorbus oriented - having been Superintendent of the coach-building and motorbus sections of the BCT - and he was instrumental in changing the policy of replacing trams by trolleybuses to one of replacing them by motorbuses. Following his appointment very few tram routes were converted to trolleybus operation.

The number of passengers carried had peaked in 1945 at 257 million (of which 155 million, or 60.31 per cent travelled by tram), and from then passenger numbers declined every year; linked to this was the rise in private car ownership in the early 1950s. The resulting congestion was often blamed on the trams, which were accused of being inflexible because of their dependence on track and overhead wires. Buses, on the other hand, were said to be able to alter route at short notice.

The Transport Department did not appreciate then that the real competition lay not between different types of public transport but between public and private transport. Elaborate plans were produced for increasing the bus and trolleybus fleet to 600 vehicles and for a new depot capable of housing and maintaining them. However, neither the increased fleet nor the new depot at Windsor happened.

On 21 August 1950 the route from Castle Junction to the LMS (formerly BNCR) railway station (via Corporation Street) became bus-operated, although trams continued to serve the siding inside the station. The BNCR had become part of the London, Midland & Scottish Railway (Northern Counties Committee) in the 1920s, and by 1950 was part of the Ulster Transport Authority (UTA), although the terms 'NC Railway' and 'LMS Railway' continued to be used on bus destination screens until recently.

By 1951 the policy of tramcar abandonment was well advanced, although 237 trams remained 'on the books'. The only routes operated by trams at June 1951 were Ligoniel, Ballygomartin, Springfield, Malone Road, Balmoral and Queen's Road. The depots at Falls Road, Antrim Road (Salisbury Avenue) and Knock had closed, and only

Ardoyne, Sandy Row, Mountpottinger and Shore Road were operational. To speed up total abandonment the department bought 100 new Daimler CVG6 buses with bodywork by the local firm of Harkness Coachbuilders, and 100 second-hand utility Daimlers from London Transport, all but 18 of which entered service with their original bodies, and which were also rebodied by Harkness in 1955-6. The 200 Daimlers entered service during 1952 and 1954 specifically on tram replacement duties, and many of them remained in service until the early 1970s.

Almost since the start of horse trams in Belfast, the main depot, repair works and Head Office was situated at Sandy Row. Just after the war the administrative section outgrew the premises there and new office accommodation was found nearby at Utility Street on the Donegall Road. Once the General Manager and Senior Staff moved in, the new offices acquired the nickname 'Futility Street'!

Belfast trams had an excellent safety record, but on 12 February 1946 a tram 'escaped' at Cliftonville terminus and headed down hill. It gathered speed and by the time it reached the bottom of Cliftonville Road was going at over 40 miles per hour (according to the *Daily Mail* account). The car jumped the points and crashed into a bootmaker's shop next door to the Phoenix public house on the Antrim Road. Fortunately no one was seriously hurt.

In July 1951 the Stranmillis tramcar service was replaced by buses, and in November the same fate befell the Malone Road route. In November 1952 the Ballygomartin, Balmoral and Springfield routes were all converted to bus operation, although trams continued to provide a rush-hour service to Mackie's factory on the Springfield Road, and to Windsor on the Lisburn Road.

By 1953 all that was left were Ligoniel via Crumlin Road, Ligoniel via Shankill Road and Queen's Road, and from February of that year buses gradually replaced trams on a journey-by-journey basis. By October trams were reduced to rush-hour services only, and the official Last Tram Procession took place on Saturday 28 February 1954.

On that day 12 Chamberlain cars travelled in convoy from Queen's Road via Station Street, Queen's Bridge, Ann Street, Victoria Street, High Street, Castle Street, Royal Avenue, North Street, Peter's Hill, Shankill Road and Woodvale Road to Ardoyne depot. As is usual for these commemorations, civic dignitaries were present and special tickets were issued to mark the occasion.

The reasons given for the policy of abandoning the trams (high cost relative to trolleybuses and inflexibility of movement) were among those deployed to support the decision in 1958 to abandon the trolleys in favour of motorbuses! More recently double-deck buses have been phased out in Belfast, and with the exception of a small number of vehicles used for specialist work, double-deckers have become candidates for 'A nostalgic look. . .' in their own right.

What is left?

At the time of writing (1994) not a great deal remains 'on the ground' to remind us of the Belfast trams. The most important items to survive are the three preserved tramcars, horse car 118, ex-horse car 249 and Chamberlain 357, which are currently in storage with the Ulster Folk and Transport Museum at Cultra, though not currently open to the public. There are plans to open a 'Road' exhibition on the Cultra site on a similar scale to the recently opened 'Rail' gallery. As part of the strive for authenticity, the Museum has acquired a number of genuine tram rails and 'square setts' from Knock depot, and it is their intention to re-create a Belfast street scene in which the trams can be seen in their natural habitat; it is hoped that this will open in late 1995 or early 1996. It is also intended to mount an interpretive display of Belfast transport using the Museum's collection of tickets, uniforms and photographs.

The Museum also has a beautiful model of a Belfast Standard Red open-topper, built around 1910 in Sandy Row Works; at present it is displayed in the foyer of the Administrative Offices. There is also a magnificent collection of photographs in the Museum library taken by W. A. Green around 1910. Besides over 50 street scenes of trams, there is a series of views of tram building in Sandy Row Works.

Of the original eight Belfast depots six are still there in varying degrees of structural soundness. Lisburn Road began life as a horse tram depot and did not make the transition to electric traction. It was used for storing various Corporation vehicles over the years, including Welfare Department minibuses and the Lord Mayor's Rolls. The depot is still there, complete with a small but genuine piece of horse-tram track.

Shore Road is also standing, although derelict and bricked up after many years service as an electricity sub-station. Antrim Road (Salisbury Avenue) served a similar function and is there yet. Falls was converted to trolleybuses, then motorbuses and continues in operation today.

The former depot at Knock was also used by the electricity department for many years, and until removed by the Ulster Folk and Transport Museum, had quite a lot of trackwork including a very nice depot fan. Ardoyne depot was also converted to motorbuses, but was closed by Citybus (the successor to BCT) very recently. The fabric of the building is standing - but only just! Sandy Row and Mountpottinger have been demolished and all traces obliterated. The former Cavehill & Whitewell depot at Glengormley, which was never used by Belfast trams, was demolished very recently.

There are a few original tram traction poles in various parts of the city. Belfast Zoo, itself a former transport department responsibility, still uses tram poles for lighting purposes in Bellevue, and there are several traction poles in a yard in Middlepath Street. There is one tram pole supporting a light in the City Hall gardens. On the 'plateau' at Bellevue there is plaque in honour of Andrew Nance, General Manager 1881-1916.

Surprisingly there are still a few old tram bodies in fields and farms around Northern Ireland, but they are generally in poor condition. However, there are tram rails buried under the road surface in various parts of the city which sometimes emerge during roadworks. In Antrim Road, near Bellevue, the rails were allowed to remain 'in situ' to help prevent subsidence.

The future

At present there are proposals by Northern Ireland Railways for the creation of a light rail line by conversion of the

Bangor suburban railway, street operation in the City Centre and a new alignment to Andersonstown. These are included in a wider study by the Department of the Environment on the future of the city centre. Perhaps Belfast might get a Metrolink like Manchester or a Supertram like Sheffield. At least the return of the tram is not as improbable as it once was. Fingers crossed!

Tickets

During the entire period of tram operation in Belfast - over 80 years - the Bell Punch system of tickets was used. Essentially there was a range of tickets, colour-coded for each fare, which conductors issued in return for the appropriate money. These were held in a rack, and before being issued to the passenger the ticket was inserted into a ticket machine and had a hole punched in it.

The location of the hole relative to the text printed on the ticket indicated whether the ticket was issued 'IN' to the city centre; 'OUT' from the centre; or 'CROSSTOWN'. Two other elements completed the financial checking system. The first was the waybill - essentially a return of tickets sold on each journey, which it was mandatory for the conductor to fill in regularly. The second element was the travelling Inspectors, whose two duties were to protect the department from fraud from the public and to protect the department from fraud from the staff.

The Bell Punch was designed in such a way as to accept only one ticket at a time; to ring a bell each time a ticket was punched; to register the number of punch holes made by the machine on a 'non-get-attable' mechanical counter; and to retain the clippings for counting in the event of a dispute. This system, incidentally, was used in most cities of any size in the UK. While not completely foolproof, it did require a high degree of collusion to sustain regular and substantial fraud.

The 'Ultimate' system was introduced on a trial basis in 1952 on trams working out of Ardoyne depot. Apart from a brief trial of a TIM (Ticket Issuing Machine) in 1933, the 'Ultimate' was the first machine to issue tickets mechanically in Belfast. The machine held five rolls of tickets, pre-printed with fares and serial numbers - about half the size of the Bell Punch ones. It had five mechanical counters; however, four registered only double issues of tickets, while the fifth recorded the total number of tickets issued.

This arrangement allowed statistics to be kept on the number of tickets sold at nine different values, which together with the information from the waybill allowed very detailed information about travel patterns to be extracted. An example of the way in which this was achieved would have been to put in tickets, say, to the values of 2d, 3d, 5d, 7d and 8d. From the serial numbers, the numbers sold of each of these values can easily be calculated. Using the special button, the four counters would have recorded the number of double issues at, say 4d, 6d, 10d and 1s 2d, while a check would have been provided by the fifth counter, which registered the total number of tickets sold.

Examples of tickets from both the Bell Punch and the Ultimate ticket systems are included later in the book.

FLEET SUMMARY

THIS is not intended to be a definitive fleet list - it is only a summary and has been included for two reasons. The first is to enable the reader to identify the trams in the photographs with the Class to which they belong, and the second is to give an idea of the increase in seating capacity, motor power and general development over the years from 1905 to 1935 when the last new cars entered service.

1-170

These trams were built by the Brush Electrical Engineering Company of Loughborough. The first cars were ready about July 1905 and the remainder arrived in Belfast in time for the opening of the newly electrified service in December. They were open-topped four-wheelers that accommodated 22 passengers downstairs on longitudinal seats and 32 upstairs on reversible 'garden' seats.

Two Westinghouse 200 35 hp motors were mounted on Brill 21E 6 ft 6 in wheelbase trucks (although 45 cars had Brush copies of the Brill trucks).

There were three large plate glass windows along the side, and doors at each end of the saloon. In general they were very similar to cars supplied to many other operators at the beginning of the century. The red livery was retained from horse car days and the Class became known as 'Standard Reds'.

From 1907 onwards the entire batch was fitted with top covers, which greatly increased the number of passengers, and revenue, in wet weather. They retained their open ends - because Andrew Nance firmly believed that it was healthier for the motormen! However, while most cars received top-deck saloons that were rather shorter than those on the bottom deck, a small number of trams were equipped with saloons that were the same length; among those so treated were fleet numbers 18, 43, 80, 110, 119 and 170.

201-250

In 1905 five of the best horse cars were scheduled for conversion to electric traction, but when stripped down they were found to be in such good condition that it was decided to convert 50 instead. Initially the cars were designed with a short canopy, which meant that the top deck was noticeably shorter than the lower one, and early photographs clearly show that the ex-horse cars were quite different in appearance from the Standard Reds. The seating capacity was 20 downstairs and 28 on the top deck. They were also painted red.

Initially these cars were equipped with motors identical to the 1-170 batch, though mounted on Brill 21E 5 ft 6 in wheelbase trucks.

The majority of the cars were altered to conform more closely with the Standards and also had top covers fitted within a short while. The longer top deck increased the upstairs seating to 30. However, 244-250 inclusive, although revamped to look like Standards, never received top covers. In later years they were used for excursion work in the summer.

171-192 and 251-291

These were built by the Corporation in Sandy Row between about 1908 and 1913. They were very similar to the Standard Reds and it is believed that they received top covers from the start. Alone of the batch, 182 received a 'long top' saloon. The fleet numbers were allocated 'either end' of the 'Cavehill & Whitewell' trams (of which more below). The cars that received 'long top' saloons were 171-178 and 181-182.

193-200

This small group of eight cars was acquired from the Cavehill & Whitewell Company in 1911. C&W 1-5 were built by Brush in 1905 on Brush AA trucks, while the other three were from a batch of 1906 Brush cars on Lycett & Conaty radial trucks. The cars were put into service with the Corporation as soon as they could be modified to look and behave as much like the Belfast Standard Reds as possible. They were fitted with trucks and motors similar to those already in service with the Standard cars. One feature that did betray the true origins of C&W cars was that they retained five ceiling panels inside as compared with the three found on 'proper' Belfast trams.

292-341

James Moffett, the General Manager, ordered 50 new trams in 1920, which were again built by Brush to a comparatively modern design. They were totally enclosed, fitted with seating for 68 (26 in the lower saloon and 42 upstairs). *Tramway and Railway World* - the trade paper of the tramway industry - still referred to 'upstairs' and 'downstairs' as 'outside' and 'inside' - a hangover from the open-top days in the early years of the century! The first few were delivered in December 1921 and the remainder in 1922.

The 'Moffetts' were initially fitted with special gear for use with trailers, in case the Corporation should ever wish to use them; in the event they never did. Although the cars were fitted with more powerful motors (40 hp at the start), there was a feeling that they were somewhat underpowered for the additional weight of larger vehicles and a greater number of passengers. The Brush Peckham pendulum P22 four-wheel trucks originally fitted had a 7 ft 6 in wheelbase. These cars had several other innovations:

Better wooden seats
Passenger-operated buzzers and conductor-operated bells
A window winding gear that operated all four top-deck side windows simultaneously, and was supposed to be used only by the conductor; these lasted throughout their life
A small door under each stair to speed up unloading at Castle Junction
Route number boxes in the front upstairs saloon

Initially painted red, in the early 1930s the majority of the Moffetts were rebuilt with 50 hp motors, cushioned seats and fitted with air brakes. The 'Castle Junction' exit door was removed at this time and the dashes were carried right round flush with the sides. As they returned to service the rebuilt cars were repainted Princess blue and white.

342-391

The 'Chamberlains' were delivered from 1930. The main batch of 40 was built by Brush of Loughborough and the remaining ten by the Service Motor Works in Belfast. They were equipped with 50 hp motors and seated 68 passengers, 24 downstairs and 44 upstairs, the majority of seats being of the transverse variety and finished with handsome leather upholstery. The trams were mounted on Maley & Taunton four-wheel swing-link trucks with a wheelbase of 8 feet. They were delivered in the new blue and white livery.

In some ways the Chamberlains were slightly extended editions of the 'Rebuilds'. Apart from the fleet numbers they could easily be distinguished by their four side windows on each deck as compared with three on the Rebuilds.

Interestingly the Chamberlains remained in service right to the end, outlasting the younger McCrearys. It is a purely personal, subjective and totally biased opinion, but I think that the Belfast Chamberlains were among the finest trams in the UK.

392-441

The last new cars delivered to Belfast were the 'McCrearys' in 1935. Streamlined, modern looking and very comfortable, they were very different from anything Belfast had seen before. The seating layout and capacity was similar to the Chamberlains and they were also fitted with two 50 hp motors mounted on the tried and tested Maley & Taunton 8-foot-wheelbase swing-link trucks.

Twenty trams (392 and 423-441) were built by the English Electric Company, and 30 (393-422) by the Service Motor Works in Belfast in a very similar specification. Detailed differences included the fact that the English Electric cars were a slightly darker blue than the Belfast-built ones. Cars built by the Service Motor Works had their headlights in the low position (about halfway up the dash), while the English Electric trams' headlights were near the top of the dash. Only the English Electric cars had the direction indicators fitted at each end of the car. As these trams were the only vehicles in Belfast so fitted, drivers of other vehicles were not used to the lights and they were blamed for a number of minor accidents. In time they fell into disuse. Finally, for the real connoisseur, the destination blinds supplied with the English Electric cars had 'GREGAGH' instead of 'CREGAGH' and 'SHANKHILL' in mistake for 'SHANKILL'!

Rebuilds

From 1929 the Corporation rebuilt 20 Standard Red cars by totally enclosing both decks, upgrading the seats, uprating the motors to 40hp (although several cars had 50 hp motors fitted for a while) and repainting them Princess blue and white. Thirty further cars were rebuilt to similar specifications by Service Motor Works during 1932. The fleet numbers of the cars were: 21, 22, 31, 35, 78, 123, 159, 164, 186 and 251-291 inclusive. The first car out of the works (and the first blue tram in Belfast) was 164.

Stores Van 8

No 8 was built in 1931 after the Standard Red of the same number was withdrawn. It had a Brill 5 ft 6 in wheelbase truck. The body may have been supplied by H. M. S. Catherwood, but is more likely to have been built by the Corporation in Sandy Row.

A

Built by Mountain & Gibson in 1906, 'A' was a brown water car, and was in service 1906-1942.

B

Also built by Mountain & Gibson in 1906, 'B' was dark green and retired in 1932.

THE CITY CENTRE

THIS comprises the area bounded by Donegall Street, Albert Memorial, Victoria Street, May Street, Howard Street, College Square East, Wellington Place, Donegall Place and Royal Avenue.

With the exception of Castle Street, very little trackwork had been abandoned by 1945; indeed, 1945 marked the year in which trams carried their largest number of passengers ever - over 155 million, or more than 60 per cent of the total passengers carried by the Department. So, in spite of the loss of route mileage, trams still played the major role in public passenger transport in Belfast.

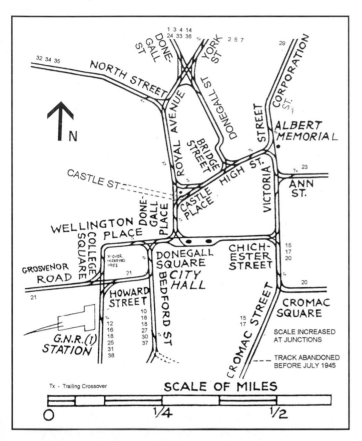

Left Belfast City Centre tramway routes in July 1945.

Below A fine view of McCreary 433 in Castle Place, taken by Roy Brook in August 1953. The tram has obviously had a bad bash, but appears nevertheless to be fit for service. At any rate it is well laden, mainly with shipyard workers heading for Queen's Road, although the bespectacled man about to board may well be on 'the staff'. In those days a person's dress was a fairly reliable guide to the nature of his or her employment.

The building occupied by the Belfast Bank (later absorbed by the Northern Bank) is still there, but currently used by the Woolwich Building Society. Robb's department store, which started in the bow-fronted building around 1860 and had expanded right down the block to Lombard Street by 1890, was demolished in 1988 and replaced by Donegall Arcade. *Roy Brook*

Above Chamberlain 365 and Moffett 322 in Castle Place in August 1952. Although the street is fairly traffic free, there are a lot of pedestrians about, probably doing their shopping. 365 is heading for the Queen's Road, about to pick up a load of shipyard workers for the journey home, while 322 is bound for the Crumlin Road fairly empty.

The large four-storey Woolworth/Burton building complete with massive top-floor cafe, directly behind the two trams, is where the young John Cole (who contributed our Foreword) occasionally sought relief from school lunches. Although superficially changed at ground-floor level, the building remains at the corner of High Street and Corn Market. It was built in 1929 replacing the famous Forster Green's tea merchants. The car on the left is a Ford Prefect. *Roy Brook*

Below This photograph was taken in January 1994 from the same spot and demonstrates that the intervening 50 years have not made all that much difference to this side of Castle Place and High Street. Woolworth and Burton still share their building, although with a modernised ground floor. The 1885 building on the corner, owned for many years by tobacconist Kelly & Leahy, was replaced in about 1970 by the almost featureless four-storey red mosaic building currently occupied by the Dolcis shoe company.

Castle Buildings (1904-7) - with the arched windows - above Connors and Wallis on the right, has been cleaned and is still very much there, although the ground floor tenancies have changed. *Mike Maybin*

Right Photographed in strong sunlight, unfortunately creating something of a shadow, Chamberlain 385 is seen in Castle Place in August 1953. Bound for Queen's Road, with no route number displayed, the tram is looking rather sorry for itself. The Inspectors' hut (sometimes unkindly referred to as 'The Tramwaymen's Dance Hall') is just behind 385.

The trolleybus on the left is turning right from Royal Avenue into Castle Street, heading for the Glen Road (a short branch opened off the Falls Road in February 1952). The bus to the right of 385 shows its destination as 'Springfield Road', a route on which the trams had been replaced the previous autumn. The 'KEEP LEFT' sign is unusual in that it makes an exception for trams!

The massive 'Bank Buildings' in the left background and the Provincial Bank of Ireland to the right are still there, though known occupied by Primark and First Trust Bank respectively. Although the building containing 'The Fifty Shilling Tailors' is still there, it is now occupied by Clarke's Shoes. Perhaps the former occupant has succumbed to inflation?
Roy Brook

Centre Compared to the previous photograph, this contemporary (1994) view of the same area is little changed. The facades of the Bank Buildings and the Provincial Bank denote new ownership in a very genteel fashion. The traffic island and tramway hut have disappeared, reflecting the pedestrianisation of the central area. Citybus, however, maintains a presence with its kiosk, and new trees contribute to the general upgrading of the City Centre during the last few years.
Mike Maybin

Right On 6 June 1953 Chamberlain 366 is set for the Queen's Road, though appears to have forgotten to have its route number changed - 57 was used for Ligoniel via Shankill Road at that time (and still is).

We now have a better view of the two main buildings in the background. The Bank Buildings was rebuilt in 1900 to the design of W. H. Lynn from a much smaller building originally established about 1885. The narrow street opposite is Castle Street, leading to the Falls Road, and a trolleybus can just be seen, retaining its rear destination display (these were phased out very shortly after the date of this photograph). The bunting around the Bank Buildings and the Union flag flying over the Provincial Bank are in honour of the Coronation. *John Price*

Left Just after the war most towns in Northern Ireland were keen to erect memorials to those who died, and in Belfast three unrebuilt Standard Reds due for scrapping were pressed into service as temporary offices and collection centre on the bomb site at the corner of Bridge Street and High Street. The advertisement on the wall for Francis Curley (established 1869) represents a firm still very much in business today, having survived not only the Luftwaffe but also the terrorist. The photograph was taken in January 1950.

When the area was rebuilt, the opportunity was taken to upgrade Bridge Street to a dual carriageway, and the site is now part of the wider street. *John H. Meredith*

Centre left Even by 1952, when this shot was taken, High Street, one of Belfast's most prestigious thoroughfares, was still gas-lit - albeit by very elegant equipment! 'Rebuild' 259 is making for the Crumlin Road, having just come from the shipyard on an evening works special. The trolley-bus overhead wiring can just be seen at the top right of the photograph - a by-pass loop has been installed to allow buses on different routes to overtake each other.

The bomb damage on the left-hand side of Alex Sloan's wallpaper shop can be clearly seen, while that on the right may be identified by the 'For Sale' board at the corner of Victoria Street. The Albert Hotel stood to the left of Alex Sloan's until the 1941 Blitz; the site is now occupied by office blocks. The Transport & General Workers' Union building is now on the right, while Alex Sloan's itself has now become the Ulster Sports Club The advertisement for Ovaltine on the side of the building is still relevant today, while regretfully that for the Mayfair Cinema is not.

The van to the extreme left beside the gas lamp is a Ford 5 cwt, the car parked outside Sloan's shop is a Jowett Javelin, while the other two cars are a Daimler and an Austin. At least three of the four famous names are still with us. *Roy Brook*

Left Union Jacks proudly fly over the Northern Bank to celebrate the Coronation - the picture was taken in June 1953. McCreary 411 is making for Queen's Road shortly after the Queen's Square/Donegall Quay/Ann Street/Victoria Street area was turned into a one-way traffic scheme in a clockwise direction. The problem was that the tram track went down Victoria Street against the new traffic flow. Since the trams were due to be scrapped in a few months it was not worth relocating the track, so a series of short-term traffic measures was put into operation.

Trolleybuses were re-routed with the traffic flow and their overhead relocated to accommodate this (the 'NO ENTRY' sign at the entrance to Queen's Square has the words 'EXCEPT TROLLEYBUSES' painted on). Trams, however, continued to turn right from High Street into Victoria Street, but were protected by a special phase in the traffic signals and a 'TURN LEFT' sign to which were added the words 'EXCEPT TRAMS'. *John Price*

Right I have to admit that this photograph of Royal Avenue does not fall into the post-1945 period! However, I have included it to give a flavour of Belfast in about 1902. It is quite remarkable that there is relatively little change between this photograph and the next, with McCreary 429. The main sweep of buildings to the left-hand side is very similar, but the three-storey brick building (known as Palace Chambers) in the distance at the corner of North Street was replaced by the Portland stone Art Deco building of the Bank of Ireland in 1928-30.

There are at least three horse trams in the picture, with number 12 advertising Castlereagh Whisky and Murray's Mellow Mixture tobacco; I don't believe that either product has survived. By this time the horse trams were all double deck with 'garden' seats on top, so called to distinguish them from the earlier 'knifeboard' seats, which were simply long seats running from front to back on which the passengers faced sideways to the direction of travel.

The trams were liberally equipped with destination and route information. There were two roller blind destination boxes front and back and two more on the sides just below roof level. In addition there were two destination boards at the front and back above the advertising boards, together with a route board on the centre of each side at waist level. All lettering was black on white. The elegant lamp fitting in the middle of Castle Junction with its four hanging globes lasted well into electric tram days, and the sign reads 'TO CASTLE PLACE'. *Lawrence Collection, National Library of Ireland*

Centre right This photograph of McCreary 429, looking up Royal Avenue from Castle Junction, was taken by Roy Brook in August 1952. The 'high' position of the headlights confirms that 429 was built by English Electric. There are also two trolleybuses and a Moffett (alas all unidentified) in the far background.

The 'skate' for operating the points (frogs) in the trolleybus overhead wiring can be seen on the nearside of the pair of 'into town' overhead wires. The nearer of the two skates on the 'into town' tram wire - it looks like two curly insulators - is in fact for operating traffic lights.

The dark building behind the tram is the Ulster Reform Club, although the ground floor is occupied at present by a building society. The Club was built in the mid-1880's as part of the larger redevelopment of the old Hercules Street into what is now Royal Avenue. However, the Grand Central Hotel and the General Post Office have been replaced by Castle Court - a new shopping arcade. The Grand Central Hotel originally opened about 1892 and closed in the 1960s, although it was occupied by the Army until the end of 1980, with the Army's nerve centre in the former bridal suite (as Marcus Patton says in *Central Belfast* (1993)); it was used for shops briefly before its demolition. The General Post Office was opened in August 1886 and extended in 1896 and 1909. It too was demolished in the 1980s. *Roy Brook*

Right The same view in January 1994 shows the replacement of the Grand Central Hotel and the General Post Office by Castle Court. Apart from pedestrianisation and the inevitable change in street furniture the view is entirely recognisable. *Mike Maybin*

Above Chamberlain 362 is seen further along Royal Avenue, again looking away from Castle Junction. The car is bound for Marlborough Park on the Lisburn Road, a short working of the Balmoral route. Also visible behind are a McCreary and a Chamberlain.

For the technically minded, trolleybus 155 (GZ 8519) on the left is a Guy BTX with GEC electrical equipment and Harkness 68-seater bodywork. The vehicle, which was new in 1949, is *en route* for Carr's Glen, an extension to the former Cliftonville tram route; it lasted in service until 1965. By the date of this photograph - 12 August 1952 - it had been decided to dispense with the rear destination displays on buses and trolleybuses, though 155 was one of the later converts.

The photograph illustrates very well one of the disadvantages of the traditional city tram - arrangements for passenger boarding and alighting. Most British urban tramway systems had the track in the centre of the roadway, a legacy of earlier days before motor traffic. In practice cars could only overtake moving trams on the inside. When the tram stopped to allow passengers to board or alight, as in this photograph, the motor traffic also had to stop. Trams were blamed as a major cause of traffic disruption and this was one of the reasons given for their demise in the British Isles in the 1950s. However, a very different climate obtains today as evidenced by Manchester's very successful Metro and Sheffield's Supertram. The motor car in question is a late-1940s Ford Prefect and the light coloured car on the left is a Standard Vanguard. *R. J. S. Wiseman*

Below left Captured by Roy Marshall on a sunny day in May 1952 is Chamberlain 361 in Donegall Place. It is *en route* for Balmoral and although no 'via' boards are carried, the route number 60 suggests the route to be via Shankill Road and Great Victoria Street. Unusual also is the 'via' blind box at the top of the second window from the door in the lower saloon which also appears to be unused. Behind 361 is an unidentified Moffett, easily distinguished from the Chamberlain by the position of the front destination box (located above the window level), the side-opening lower deck quarter lights (as opposed to the bottom-hinged ones on the Chamberlains) and the lack of top-deck quarter lights. Just visible beyond the Moffett is a trolleybus, while behind it is one of the newly acquired wartime London Transport Daimlers, still in the original utility body.

The 'Brands' sign is a reminder of Brand's Emporium (Ulster Arcade). Just to the left of Brand's and behind the Chamberlain is Thornton's, also demolished in the Blitz but quickly rebuilt into a five-storey department store. As a small boy my Saturday treat was a visit to the top floor, all of which was given over to toys! The gap is now filled by a C&A store that has since expanded and now includes the Thornton Building.

The four-storey building with the French-style Mansard roof was formerly the Imperial Hotel. At the turn of the century it was one of the most famous, modern and expensive in Northern Ireland, but by the date of this photograph had become a British Sailors' Society hostel. *Roy Marshall*

Right Moffett 319 was just about to turn right from Donegall Place into Castle Place when photographed in August 1952. It is bound for Queen's Road, probably on a shipyard special. This particular car lasted until 1953, though many of its contemporaries were scrapped in 1952. Nevertheless, this was still over 30 years service!

Anderson & McAuley's department store is still there, though it has just ceased trading. Donegall Chambers (built about 1932) and Fountain House, designed by Young & Mackenzie in the mid-1930s, are also still there today. The impressive building at the south end of Donegall Place is, of course, Belfast City Hall. It was opened in 1906 on a site previously occupied by the White Linen Hall, from which Linenhall Street got its name. The City Hall remains the centre for Belfast's local government.

The AEC trolleybus is bound for Fortwilliam Park, a short working of the Whitehouse route. There are three further trams, a trolleybus and a bus in the background. The motor car on the left is a Morris Oxford, while the lorry on the right, just peeping out from behind the front tram, is a Bedford. *Roy Brook*

Centre right Taken about 1951, this photograph shows Moffetts 302 and 320 in Donegall Place, about to turn right into Donegall Square North heading for Malone Road and Stranmillis Road respectively.

The Belfast Corporation trolleybus (15) was the first of the production AECs delivered from 1940. Within the next year or so the decision had been taken to save money by omitting the legend 'BELFAST CORPORATION' from the sides of buses and trolleybuses. Brown's furniture van can be seen squeezed between the two tramcars. The City Centre is still gas-lit. *W. J. Wyse*

Below right Travelling in the opposite direction, Chamberlain 343 is heading towards Ligoniel via Crumlin Road in 1951, having got the green light to turn left from Donegall Square North into Donegall Place. The bus in the background, about to turn left out of Donegall Place, is going to the Northern Counties Railway Station via Corporation Street. Buses had replaced trams on the route the previous year, but the route was eventually abandoned altogether as the redevelopment of the Corporation Street area (known as Sailortown) gradually changed the nature of the district from residential houses to commercial property.

The trolleybus further down Chichester Street in the distance still has a full rear destination display, indicating that it is on the Stormont route. Shortly after this photograph was taken, BCT vehicles had the rear destination screens painted out and later panelled over.

The Capstan advertisement on the bus reflected a brand of cigarettes very popular 40 years ago, and Butlin's holiday camps, as advertised on the tram, are still pulling them in! There is an Austin 16 to the extreme left following a Ford Anglia, the NZ registration indicating its County Londonderry origins. *Alan B. Cross*

Left A study of McCreary 439 at the loading island in Donegall Square North, one of the batch built by English Electric, with the direction indicators and stop lamp still in situ, and with Chamberlain 370 not far behind and the 'tail end' of a BCT bus just visible. There are few pieces of evidence to date this photograph, but the route numbers on the trams put it some time before February 1951 - possibly much earlier. The McCreary is bound for Malone Road while the Chamberlain is heading to Balmoral.

The white building in the background is, of course, the City Hall, opened in 1906, while that to the left is Donegall Square Methodist Church (opened 20 June 1847). *C. Flewitt*

Centre left Again, unfortunately the precise date of this photograph is not known to me, but I would estimate 1950 - certainly no later than February 1951. Moffett 296 is turning left into Donegall Place on the 32 route to Ballygomartin, while a McCreary can just be seen to the left passing Robinson & Cleaver's building. Daimler bus 251 (GZ 4005) of 1947 vintage, on the right, is on the Sydenham route and has not yet got the 'small route number box' treatment.

In 1951 there was a major re-organisation of route numbers with the intention of allocating the sequence 51-99 to buses. As the route number blinds fitted to buses at that time had digits 15 inches high, a blind with 49 numbers would have been well over 60 feet long; it would have been very heavy and time-consuming to wind from one end to the other. Consequently the top and bottom thirds of the aperture were blanked out and blinds with figures about 5 inches high were fitted. Although this arrangement was much more easily managed from the point of view of the platform crews, obviously some legibility was sacrificed.

An unidentified 1950 Guy is on the Oldpark service, and the whole tranquil scene suggests a quiet Sunday morning. The quaint construction with the spires just behind the Guy is the Ocean Building, designed by Young & Mackenzie and completed in 1902. The statue on the plinth in Chichester Street, which causes the tram track to take evasive action, is a memorial to the victims of the Titanic disaster of 1912. *H. B. Priestley*

Left In May 1994 Donegall Square North is still dominated by Robinson & Cleaver's building and what is now the Pearl Assurance building. The former no longer operates as a single retail shop, but has been converted to individual shops and offices while retaining the famous facade. Imperial House, the mid-1930s four-storey building to the right of the Pearl building in the old photograph, is still there, though almost invisible behind the trees. The former 'Water Office' building to the right of Robinson & Cleaver has been purchased by Marks & Spencer, and although completely renovated inside, the 19th-century facade has been preserved. The Titanic Memorial has been moved to the safety of the City Hall, as it proved somewhat of a traffic hazard when the one-way scheme was implemented in 1958. *Mike Maybin*

BELFAST TRAMS SINCE 1945

Above In this 1952 view of Donegall Square North McCreary 410 is just turning out of Donegall Place *en route* to Mountpottinger Depot. Two unidentified trolleybuses are also in the picture. It was not until July 1958 (four years after the trams were abandoned) that the one-way traffic scheme based on the City Hall came into force; until then trolleybuses bound for routes crossing the Albert Bridge took on their passengers at Donegall Square East and left via May Street.

The 'black box' on the nearside trolleybus overhead wire just slightly ahead of the pole carried by the man in overalls was a contact skate, which allowed the overhead frog to be changed automatically. By 'coasting' through the contactor the trolleybus did not operate the frog and the trolleys followed one path; by pressing the power (accelerator) pedal at the same time as applying the handbrake lightly while passing under the contactor, the additional power required energised a solenoid and changed the frog.

An old-style concrete telephone kiosk can just be glimpsed behind the traction pole and the elegant gas light is discernible among the forest of poles. The private car parked beside the lamp is a Jaguar, while the one on the move is a pre-war Wolseley. There is a Bedford van on the right of the McCreary, while the rear end of a Ford can just be seen at the extreme right of the picture. *Roy Brook*

Right In many ways this photograph for me epitomises childhood memories of Belfast. Although I don't have a precise date for it, judging from the route numbers on the tram and bus it was probably taken between February 1951 and July 1952. Moffett 316 is *en route* to Malone Road via Great Victoria Street. So is the bus, but its terminus at that time was at 'The Dub' and the route served Stanmillis Road as well.

The 'STAGE' sign in the top left-hand corner marked the tram loading island designed to improve passenger safety at a very busy tram stop, but unfortunately there were few other examples in Belfast. The old style 'NO WAITING' sign and former pedestrian crossing before the days

of 'zebra' road markings are visible just below the triangular YMCA sign.

The five-storey 'Athletic Stores' on the right in Wellington Place, established in 1885, was bombed by the IRA in the 1970s and the building demolished; it was later replaced by a glass and concrete office block. The Stores itself continued trading in a variety of places including, at the time of writing, Queen Street, but not on the previous scale. Just outside the Stores a Ford lorry is parked, while nearer the photographer a Morris Commercial is waiting.

The Scottish Provident building to the left is still standing. Like so many others in the City Centre it was built between 1897 and 1902 by Young and Mackenzie. Regretfully, however, Crane's pianos (on the right at the corner of Fountain Street) was replaced by an office block for the Prudential Assurance Company in the early 1960s.

The top of the Belfast College of Technology can just be seen above the roofline of the Moffett. This large building was erected on the grounds of the Royal Belfast Academical Institution ('Inst') at the beginning of the century, and badly obscured the very fine classical front of Inst. At that time Inst badly needed the cash realised by the sale of the land. *H. B. Priestley*

Above The world famous store of Robinson & Cleaver at the corner of Donegall Place and Donegall Square North is to the right of 'Rebuild' 280 in this photograph looking towards Wellington Place taken by Roy Brook in the summer of 1952. The R&C building (though no longer a department store) and the Scottish Provident Institution visible to the left of the Titanic Memorial remain today, and another glimpse of the front of 'Inst' can be seen at the western end of Wellington Place.

The tram is headed for Mountpottinger Depot, and just to the right of the Vauxhall car is a better view of the early concrete telephone box glimpsed on the previous page. *Roy Brook*

Below Photographed in August 1952, Chamberlain 383 bound for Balmoral (via Bedford Street) approaches the loading island in Donegall Square North. A lady appears to be trying to board 363 from the wrong side, which was a fairly dangerous thing to do even in those relatively traffic-free days. A Moffett can be discerned in the background, its fleet number unfortunately obscured by pedestrians.

Relatively few of the buildings on the right of the photograph remain in this form today, with the exceptions of the Linenhall Library - the brick three-storey building at the corner of Fountain Street - and the three-storey red sandstone building next door currently occupied by the Halifax Building Society. You can just see the offices of the Bingley Building Society, in the days before it was joined by the Bradford. The lorry to the right of 363 is an Austin, owned by Thomas Hunter of Boyne Square, who, amongst other things, manufactured soap. *Roy Brook*

Above McCreary 432 heads a nice procession of vehicles north-bound along Lower Donegall Street, including trolleybus 197 (GZ 8561) - a 1950 BUT 9641 T 211 with Harkness 68-seater bodywork and GEC electrical equipment - which is on its way to Glengormley via Carlisle Circus, although the destination display helpfully adds 'BELLEVUE AND ZOOLOGICAL GDS' on the second line. Two further (unidentified) McCreary's follow and the final Transport Department vehicle is one of the early trolleybuses (1-14), identified as such by the route number box being mounted to the nearside; all the other trolleybuses had theirs on the offside. The trolleybus overhead wires divide into two pairs at this point. Those nearer the pavement are for vehicles going via Carlisle Circus, while the other pair are for buses bound for York Street.

The three/four-storey red-brick Cathedral Buildings (constructed at the turn of the century) immediately to the right of the front tramcar remains in place today, although the ground floor units are now a sandwich bar, an estate agent and a business centre. The assertion painted on the wall below the advertisements is one with which few would disagree!

Immediately behind the tram is an Austin car, while there is a Morris Minor parked outside Anderson's shop and a Velocette motorbike being ridden by the man with a beret - of course this was long before it was compulsorily for motor cyclists to wear crash helmets. *Roy Brook*

Right 'Rebuild' 282 is just passing Robinson's Hotel in Upper Donegall Street *en route* for the Crumlin Road. This was always one of the most complex tram junctions in Belfast. In addition to the Royal Avenue-York Street and Upper Donegall Street-Lower Donegall Street

links, there were links between Royal Avenue and Upper Donegall Street and between Lower Donegall Street and York Street, all of which were double tracked. Finally there was a single-track curve from Lower Donegall Street into Royal Avenue. When the Corporation came to wire for trolleybuses for the Antrim Road route it was decided that it would be easier to divert incoming trolleybuses via North Queen Street, Frederick Street and York Street. Even so the resulting tangle of traction wires was most impressive!

Duffin's and Magill's shops are no longer standing, and this corner is now occupied by the new *Belfast Telegraph* building, as is Robinson's Hotel. The car turning right from Donegall Street into Royal Avenue is a Morris 8. *Roy Brook*

Left Looking in the same direction from the other side of Lower Donegall Street, Chamberlain 354 is seen in Upper Donegall Street *en route* to the crossover in College Square East (although trams showed 'CITY HALL' on the destination blinds). Berris's furniture store on the corner of Upper Donegall Street and York Street went through a succession of owners, several of whom, like Berris's, offered inexpensive furniture on hire purchase.

The advertisement for the *Irish News* - the main Nationalist newspaper in Northern Ireland - painted on the wall of its office is no longer there, although the paper itself is in business. Interestingly the *News Letter*, the main Unionist paper, also had its office in Donegall Street until comparatively recently, and the extension to the *Telegraph* building resulted in a large frontage (albeit the side!) on Donegall Street.

The Bedford furniture lorry behind the tram belongs to the Ulster Transport Authority - a semi-state body given a near monopoly of carrying passenger and goods traffic throughout Northern Ireland, outside the Belfast area. I have been unable to identify the car outside Duffin's shop on the left, but the one on the right is an Austin A40. *Roy Brook*

Centre left Taken from as near the same viewpoint as modern traffic conditions allowed (even on a Sunday!), in January 1994, the Donegall Street Congregational Church building has been rebuilt following the Blitz of 1941. The new *Belfast Telegraph* extension can be seen on the left of the picture, while Berris's is up for sale. *Mike Maybin*

Below left Chichester Street, the location for this view of Moffett 296, was the last piece of new track laid in the City Centre and was used by only a handful of regular tramcar services until the early 1940s, when the East Belfast routes began to be converted to trolleybus operation. At this time a number of cross-town links were cut, many of those services that terminated in the City Centre using the turning loop of Victoria Street, High Street, Donegall Place and Chichester Street in both directions. 296 is seen here working the Ormeau Road service, having used the loop in an anti-clockwise direction.

Initially the whole Moffett class of 50 cars was fitted with 'via' blinds in the lower saloon, but by April 1948, when this photograph was taken, only 296 and 315 retained them. The motorbus is on the Cherryvalley route (6), while the trolleybus on the extreme left is returning to the City Hall from the Bloomfield route (20). His Majesty's Stationery Office is still there, though now renamed the Government Bookshop, but has been completely rebuilt, as has the building to the left of it. An old Ford lorry can be seen between the bus and the tram. *D. G. Coakham*

Above A goodly selection of trams at the junction of Victoria Street and Ann Street in August 1952. 'Rebuild' 159 is turning right from Ann Street into Victoria Street bound for Shankill Road via High Street, while two further 'Rebuilds' and a Chamberlain are also heading in the direction of the City Centre. The Chamberlain (advertising wallpapers and paints) is turning left into Victoria Street and is making for the City Hall via Chichester Street. Virtually all the buildings in Ann Street have disappeared, while the lone policeman directing the traffic is but a memory of happier days in Belfast. *Roy Brook*

Right A further example of a one-way system was that introduced at Cromac Square in 1953, shortly before this photograph was taken in June of that year. The traffic was re-routed clockwise via Lower May Street, Oxford Street, East Bridge Street and Cromac Street. Again the trams were not included because of their short life expectancy, and were protected against the traffic by lights with a special 'TRAMS GO' phase as shown here at the junction of Victoria Street and May Street.

Interestingly, AEC trolleybus 42 is on the Ormeau Road route, which was served by trolleybuses only from 1948 until 1958. The section of its waist-panel just ahead of the words 'BELFAST CORPORATION' (as on all the AECs) was unpainted because the hook of the trolley pole which was carried along the side of the bus scraped the paint! Later vehicles carried their trolley poles in a tube underneath the vehicle. *John Price*

Above This photograph was taken in Donegall Square West in 1951. Heavily laden 'Rebuild' 287, turning right, is *en route* for Ballygomartin. Although 287 carries a 'via' board at the bottom of the front off-side window, it is also equipped with a 'via' blind box at the top of the middle window, which for some reason appears to have fallen into disuse.

On the left of the photograph is one of the old-style telephone kiosks introduced before the War, while on the right is the Linenhall Library. The tracks curving left from Donegall Square West into Wellington Place were rarely used apart from football specials 'parked' here during matches at Windsor Park. The office block known as 'Prudential Chambers' at the corner of Fountain Street and Wellington Place (see also pages 25-6) was replaced with a rather bland five-storey concrete building, also for the Prudential Assurance Company, in the early 1960s. *Alan B. Cross*

Below This view of a rather battered Moffett 298 was taken in Donegall Square West about 1950. At that time Greencastle trams operated to Donegall Square West, and 298 is just about to reverse over the crossover. The three buses, at least two of which are Daimlers, have full destination displays at the rear and the words 'BELFAST CORPORATION' in gold-shaded black letters on the waistbands; both of these features began to disappear from about 1951. The massive one-way traffic system based on the City Hall was not introduced until July 1958. *D. W. K. Jones*

Above In the days before the City Hall became the focus for the one-way traffic scheme, buses and trams used Donegall Square in both directions. McCreary 437 is seen here making for the Springfield Road displaying the correct route number. However, a destination blind has been put into the 'via' aperture on the side and has been set at 'CRUMLIN ROAD' (which was the other end of the route). In practice this would have been unlikely to have caused much confusion given the relatively small number of tram-car routes left in 1952 when this view was taken. The 'UNLOADING STOP ONLY' sign on the right dates from before the more polite word 'ALIGHTING' was introduced in the 1960s. The old-style 'NO WAITING - SEE NOTICE BELOW' beneath it was the forerunner of the modern urban clearway signs.

Most of the buildings to the right of the tram on Donegall Square North (where the camera is pointing) have been demolished to make way for new developments, mostly of an office block nature. The car behind the McCreary is an Armstrong-Siddeley. *Roy Brook*

Right McCreary 420 about to pass over the 'square crossing' at Fisherwick junction in the early 1950s. It is on the Springfield Road-Crumlin Road route and has just been halted by the traffic lights (on black and white striped poles). The photographer is standing with his back to Howard Street looking up the vista of Grosvenor Road. Although double curves were installed from Grosvenor Road to Fisherwick Place and from Howard Street to Great Victoria Street, these were not used in normal service until shortly before the end, when Springfield cars did turn left into Fisherwick Place, as opposed to their normal route via Howard Street.

The tram is sandwiched between the Hippodrome (later known as the Odeon and New Vic) on the left of the picture and, on the right, the Ritz, at that time showing *Operation Pacific* with John Wayne; it was later known as the ABC. Recently demolished, at the time of writing it is used as a car park. The church-like building to the left is the Grosvenor Hall, built by Young and Mackenzie around 1925 and at present still standing. *H. B. Priestley*

Above Chamberlain 345 is seen in Wellington Place on the shuttle service from City Hall to Ligoniel via Crumlin Road. By this stage (August 1953) the only 'all-day' tram services still operating were Ligoniel and Queen's Road. The Ligoniel service - although showing 'CITY HALL' as the City Centre terminal point - actually went past the City Hall itself, up Wellington Place and turned left into College Square East, reversing over the newly installed crossover there. 345 has just departed from the crossover round the corner, and the photographer has his back to the City Hall. A Morris Oxford car is parked outside Florence Graham's shop. *Roy Brook*

Below Dated 6 June 1953, this view of Chamberlain 370 taken at the corner of Wellington Place and College Square East, looking towards 'Inst', shows how well Belfast tramcars were maintained right up to the end. Although slight damage is discernible on the front dash panel, the car is very well turned out given that it has already seen 20 years' service. The statue is known locally as the 'Black Man', not because of the colour of the present statue of Rev Henry Cooke, but because of an earlier statue of the Earl of Belfast whom Cooke replaced in 1876. That statue was initially bronze, being later painted black - and the name stuck.

'Inst' has received a set of gates in the meantime and Rev Cooke has since become a traffic island, but not a great deal else has changed in the last 40 years. *R. J. S. Wiseman*

Above A most unusual line-up of cars in College Square East in May 1952. McCreary 403, one of the Service-built cars, is last in a queue of at least five trams including a 'Rebuild' and three Chamberlains. The 'via' blind in the McCreary is unusual in having a three-line display.

Also in the photograph, on the extreme left, is a Belfast Corporation Daimler with Harkness bodywork headed for Ormeau Road via Great Victoria Street, and in the far background is a UTA single-decker - probably a Leyland PS 1 or 2. *H. M. Rea*

Right Taken by John Gillham on 13 June 1953, less than a year before the abandonment of trams in Belfast, this view of Chamberlain 383, together with the two interior photographs of the same car overleaf, suggests that the cars were maintained to a high standard right up to closure.

There are advertisements for City Bus Tours in both saloons, while the outside slogan attempts to persuade housewives (no need for the politically correct 'housepersons' in those days!) of the value of Crosse & Blackwell soups.

Armstrong's tobacco shop is no longer there, nor is the Kensington Hotel, which is recorded on a map as early as 1819; the Union flag was being flown in honour of

the Coronation. The ecclesiastical-looking building in the right background was (and still is) Assembly's Buildings - effectively the headquarters of the Presbyterian Church in Ireland - and is today more or less unchanged in purpose and appearance. *J. G. Gillham*

Above This upper deck view of Chamberlain 383 shows the transverse seating layout with the semi-circular inward-facing four-person seat at the front. The coloured glass with white star motif at the top of the windows somehow typifies, for me, Belfast trams.

Below The lower deck of some Chamberlains, including 383, had one column of transverse seats removed during the war in order to allow extra standing. The motorman is obviously aware that this photograph is being taken! *Both J. G. Gillham*

Right A few months before the Balmoral route was converted to buses, Moffett 307 heads down College Square East, and Chamberlain 369 is *en route* for Crumlin Road. Guy Arab 311 (MZ 7409), new in 1950, was part of a batch of 45 similar vehicles; it still retains its rear destination display and titled waistband, both of which were to disappear within the next couple of years.

The four entertainment centres in this area underwent many changes during their lifetimes. The Mayfair just to the left of the bus began life as The Kelvin in 1910, changed to The Mayfair in 1946, the News & Cartoon in 1958, the Classic in 1970 and finally closed in 1972. The Ritz (see also page 31) opened in 1936 replacing a temporary circus on the site, became the ABC in 1981 and was demolished in 1993. The Hippodrome opened in 1907, briefly called itself The Palace for a couple of years, and was known at various times as the Odeon and New Vic. The Grand Opera House, just beyond the Hippodrome, was never successful as a cinema, but is a superb venue for live entertainment. In spite of being severely damaged on several occasions by IRA bombs, the building has been brilliantly restored and as I write is due to re-open in a few weeks in time for the 1994 Christmas panto season. The large building with the tower is Assembly's Buildings.

The CZ-registered Austin 10 overtaking 369 on the inside looks a little old-fashioned beside the line-up of cars on the extreme right. *Roy Brook*

Centre right This view of Fisherwick Place from College Square East was taken in May 1994 and contrasts greatly with the August 1952 photograph. The Mayfair cinema and the Kensington Hotel next door to Assembly's Buildings have been replaced by Stokes House. The Ritz on the right has very recently been demolished and at the time of writing is a car park.

There is a series of tower blocks along Great Victoria Street and it is no longer allowed to park cars at right angles to the kerb as was the practice in 1952. College Square East has also become part of a one-way traffic scheme. *Mike Maybin*

Right A very unusual view of a McCreary 432 taken from an upstairs window in College Square East on 6 June 1953. Apart from shipyard and other works specials, the last tram route to operate in Belfast was City Centre-Ligoniel, and for the last few months cars operated to and from the City Hall, using this crossover in College Square East, a wide street with relatively little traffic. The 'via' box has a 'destination' blind in it, but as Ligoniel was one of the few places left for trams to go by this stage, little confusion ensued.

Radio Times was being advertised very widely around this time, as television broadcasting in the province was just beginning. Belfast Corporation Transport also advertised its popular City Tours on both decks of this McCreary. The low wall and railings in the background mark the boundary of the 'Inst', the Royal Belfast Academical Institution. *John Price*

EAST BELFAST

PHOTOGRAPHS in this section were taken in Ann Street, Station Street, the Belfast & County Down railway station, Bridge End, Newtownards Road, Bloomfield, Albertbridge Road, Mountpottinger Road and East Bridge Street. By 1945 the routes to Stormont, Dundonald, Castlereagh and Cregagh had been turned over to trolleybus operation.

Below **East Belfast tramway routes in July 1945.**

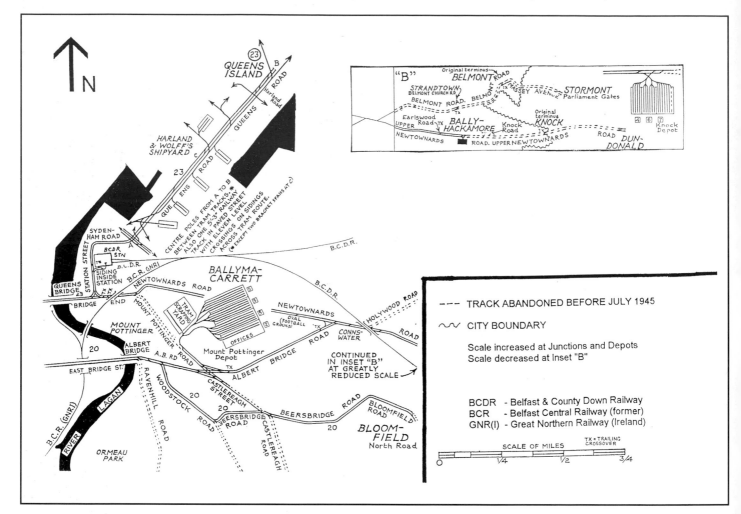

Left Leading a procession of at least 11 trams in Station Street is 22, heading for Balmoral with a large complement of homeward-bound shipyard workers. Typical of the 1950s (this is August 1952) is the paucity of private transport, although what is probably a Vespa scooter can just be seen between the tram and the bus. From other evidence the bus is one of the first post-war Daimler CWAs.

22 was one of 50 Standard Red cars rebuilt as a result of William Chamberlain's policy of modernisation in the late 1920s. This example is unusual in having all its upper deck windows the same height. The majority of the 'Rebuild' batch retained three side windows deeper than the others, and in my view were not examples of good design. *Roy Brook*

BELFAST TRAMS SINCE 1945

Right In addition to a large number of trams being required to carry the shipyard men home at night, a fleet of Corporation buses was also necessary to reach those parts of Belfast from which trams had been withdrawn. This unidentified Moffett, photographed near the top of Station Street in the early 1950s, was bound for the Shankill Road with a great many more passengers on a great many more places than officially allowed.

Belfast Corporation Daimler 268 (a Daimler CVA6) is heading for Garnerville Road. It was new to Belfast in 1947, carried a Harkness 54-seater body on Park Royal frames, and was one of a batch intended to facilitate the programme of tram replacement.

The Picturedrome cinema advertised on the billboard at the top of Station Street was situated on Mountpottinger Road, next door to the tram depot. However, it was one of the earlier casualties of the advent of television. *W. J. Wyse*

Above Car 89 cannot properly be classed as either a Standard Red or a 'Rebuild'. This photograph, taken in Station Street in 1949, shows the car fairly packed with homeward-bound shipyard workers; as happened every weeknight there is a large quantity of almost nose-to-tail Chamberlains and Standards. 89 received this experimental top covering in the early 1920s, long before the main rebuilding took place. This car remained unique in having a fully enclosed top saloon without any corresponding protection for the motorman. One result was that the motorman got much wetter than he would have done on an open Standard Red. Not surprisingly, this tram was very unpopular with the crews! *R. W. A. Jones*

Below Working the City Hall-Queen's Road service in the early 1950s, also in Station Street, is McCreary 409. Judging from the relatively light passenger loading the rush-hour has not started. Middlepath Street, visible in the left background sandwiched between the tram stage and the pub, is all that remains of this view today, and even that thoroughfare has totally changed in character from the small urban backwater shown here to the four-lane approach to the Sydenham Bypass which it is today. *R. F. Mack, courtesy A. D. Packer*

Above 'Rebuilds' were a favourite class of car to operate on 'Shipyard Specials'. 252 was originally one of the Standard Reds built by the Corporation in their Sandy Row works in the period before and during the First World War. Heavily rebuilt about 1928, they provided excellent service for over 40 years.

Unlike the tram pictured on page 36, this 'Rebuild' retained the deep centre side windows in the top-deck saloon. The majority of the 'Rebuild' Class followed this design rather than the much more elegant (in my view) design used in car 22.

A 'section feeder' is visible on the tramway overhead. It was a Board of Trade requirement that tramway routes should be divided into half-mile sections, each of which had to have an independent electrical feed. Although this was primarily a safety feature, there were operational benefits as any electrical section could be switched out in an emergency.

A UTA single-decker can just be seen in the background, while an unidentified BCT double-decker, a Scammell Scarab 6-ton 'mechanical horse', an Austin Ruby car and a Norton motor cycle are very much 1950s memories. All the buildings behind the tram have now been pulled down to facilitate major roadworks. *C. Carter*

Left A clear view of 'Rebuild' 265 taken in May 1952, also in Station Street, heading up a procession of homeward-bound cars from the Queen's Island shipyard. By 1952 there was no direct tram service from Queen's Road to Mountpottinger Depot, although trams operated in the other direction and also from the City Centre to the depot. It is probable that the motorman omitted to change the destination display. Just to the right of 265 is the section box supplying the feeder wires noted in the previous photograph. *Roy Brook*

Above Returning from a run to the Queen's Road and bound for the City Hall is Moffett 330. The use of the destination 'CITY HALL' for trams only came into operation a short time before abandonment.

When this photograph was taken the docks were working at full capacity and Northern Ireland was almost totally reliant on coal from Great Britain. As can be seen, a number of coal merchants were located in and around Queen's Quay. The Belfast & County Down Railway station's covered carriageway was rarely used by this stage, while the letters U and T can be seen on either side of the clock, standing for Ulster Transport Authority. The UTA was established in 1948 to acquire the assets of the Northern Ireland Road Transport Board (NIRTB) and the LMS(NCC) and BCD railways. The terminus station is now completely demolished.

The railway's advertisement for a one-day excursion fare to Bangor for 2s 9d harks back to a time when inflation was thought of only in terms of bicycle tyres! The road vehicles, from left to right, are a Ford 10 cwt van, a Commer and a Karrier Bantam. *Roy Brook*

Below *En route* to Queen's Road during the last year of tramcar operation, Chamberlain 371 is seen near the junction of Station Street with Queen's Quay. The BCDR station is on the right, with an Austin taxi waiting patiently outside. Although there was a crossover on the 'main line' outside the station, by the time this photograph was taken most cars terminating at the station used the tram bay in Scrabo Street. *Roy Brook*

Although this photograph was taken in 1952, 287 is looking very well turned out for a tram almost 40 years old and due to be retired within 18 months. It is well laden not only upstairs and downstairs, but outside as well! Hanging on to the bumpers of shipyard trams was a long and honourable Belfast tradition. The bus, 249 (GZ 4003), is a Daimler CVA6 new in 1947 with a Harkness 54-seater body.

249 has the route number aperture reduced by about two-thirds to take account of the larger sequence of route numbers allocated to buses in February 1951 (see page 24). *Roy Brook*

Photographed on 25 July 1951 by R. C. Jackson, 'Rebuild' 164 heads a large procession of 'Rebuilds', Moffetts and Chamberlains in preparation for the homeward trek from Queen's Island. 164, incidentally, was the first of the Standard Reds to be rebuilt into the DK1 Class, as the 'Rebuilds' were officially known. *R. C. Jackson*

'Rebuild' 257 stands at the back of another long queue of trams ready to receive the thousands of shipyard workers in a few minutes when the hooter sounds. By the time that this photograph was taken in August 1952, the tram replacement programme was well under way and this view of the line-up shows many of the cars looking very tired. Although Harland & Wolff is still operating today, the workforce is barely one-fifth of the 1952 strength, and most of those have their own cars, so there is unfortunately no equivalent large fleet of buses required. *Roy Brook*

BELFAST TRAMS SINCE 1945

Above Photographed by John Price on the occasion of the Light Railway Transport League (LRTL) tour in June 1953, Moffett 340, complete with dent on dash panel, is posed beside a railway crossing. In the early days of this century Harland & Wolff had an extensive network of private railway lines which crisscrossed the Queen's Road tram track and contributed to a rough ride on this route. As road transport developed the railway fell into disuse, but some of the track remained in place long after the tram rails had been lifted. The destination 'SPECIAL' was a blind specially made for the tour - Belfast tram destination blinds did not have this display. *John Price*

Below 'Rebuild' 123 emerges from 'County Down Ry', the BCDR station in Scrabo Street, in May 1950. It appears that the conduc-

tor has forgotten to change the rear destination blind and set the route number and 'via' screens! This was unusual, as generally in Belfast there was a very high standard of accuracy in the display of destination information.

This view is fairly uncommon - the camera is pointed towards the City Centre across the river, and the view includes some boats moored near the Queen's Bridge. The advertisements on the tram, like the entire area, regretfully no longer exist. However, Barry's amusements, advertised on the station, while no longer operating amusement arcades and pleasure gardens at Bellevue or Bangor, continue to operate at Portrush. The establishment at Bangor was located on the sea front next door to the Court House, and was run by Minnie Delino until her retirement at well over 70 years of age. *H. C. Casserley*

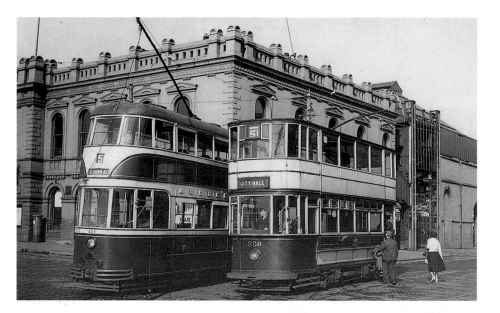

Looking in the opposite direction into Scrabo Street, Moffett 330 is seen leaving the tram bay at the BCDR station for the City Hall on a sunny day in August 1952, with McCreary 428 on its way in. 428 was one of the batch built by English Electric and can be recognised by the position of her headlamps located near the top of the dash; the locally built Service Motor Works cars' headlamps were near the centre of the dash.

The tram bay at the station was a very welcome feature, particularly on wet or cold days, and for many years trams were timetabled to meet the principal trains both here and at the Northern Counties station in York Road. *Roy Brook*

Chamberlain 386 and 'Rebuild' 256 are neatly framed between competing sets of advertisements in the tram bay at the BCDR station in May 1950. There was just enough room to swing the trolley inside the station, although the single-track bay meant that trams operated on a 'last in - first out' basis. However, it was possible to overcome this to some extent if later cars waited in the double-track section outside.

The power of advertising was obviously strongly believed in here (or at least the revenue which it provided was!). Hewitt's are no longer in Sandy Row, nor is Edith Graham in Castle Lane. However, the *Financial Times*, the *Investors' Chronicle* and the *Christian Science Monitor* are still very much around. I don't know about *Engineering* or *The Truth* - perhaps the latter only in selected areas! *H. C. Casserley*

Back out in the sunshine, a well-laden Moffett (at least on the lower deck) emerges from the entrance to the tram bay bound for the City Hall, correctly displaying route number 51. The UTA buses further down Scrabo Street are operating the railway replacement services for those lines that had been closed a few years earlier, and until recent years a faded NIRTB bus stop sign for Comber could be seen just about where the buses are in the picture. The photograph was taken in the early 1950s. *W. J. Wyse*

BELFAST TRAMS SINCE 1945

Moffett 306 has just turned right from Station Street into Scrabo Street and is about to go into the tram bay just past the gas lamp. It is not clear whether there is sufficient clearance to allow the tram to pass the van; although the track curves to the right it does not look hopeful. . . The conductor, however, does not look at all concerned! The pub to the right has long since disappeared, as have virtually all the buildings in the photograph. *J. Joyce*

Perhaps not so much a tram photograph - more a good view of the corner of the County Down Railway station showing a traction engine, a bicycle, two horses and carts and about a third of a McCreary tramcar. For many years the station was the fare stage and the sign is seen here attached to the traction pole to the left of the traction engine painted with a variety of stripes. The colours and locations of these stripes changed over the years and also included identifying section insulators and frogs (points) in the overhead line. The little van half hidden by the horses and carts is a Ford 10 cwt; the photograph was taken in 1951. *W. J. Wyse*

'Rebuild' 78, another of the few cars of this class to have 'same height' upper deck windows, returns citywards from the Queen's Road past the station. In the top of the middle window of the lower saloon can just be seen the frame of a destination box, though without any blind by this stage. In the 1930s many cars were fitted with a combined destination and route screen, but for whatever reason 'via' boards held on by brackets fitted at the bottom of the window nearest the door seemed to endure longer. *A. D. Packer*

Above Standard Red 182 heads a long procession of cars in Ann Street; they have just come from Queen's Road and are heading to various suburbs in North and West Belfast. Interestingly, with the exception of two 'Rebuilds' every car in the line is a Standard Red - there are no Moffetts, Chamberlains or McCreary's. 182 is about to turn left into Victoria Street, a relatively rare manoeuvre carried out by only a few rush-hour cars. The points for the curve were manually operated, hence the motorman with the point-iron. The tram has just overshot the points, which accounts both for the long queue of cars and the small group of people critically studying the situation.

Two trolleybuses can just be glimpsed, one in the left distance and the other returning to Castle Junction from Castlereagh, on the inside of 182. The photograph was taken on 16 May 1948 and the camera is looking towards Queen's Bridge. *W. A. Camwell*

Left On the same day, this view shows Belfast Corporation bus 99 (CZ 7010), a Dennis Lancet 31-seater single-decker fitted with a Service Motor Works body. Originally new in 1935, 99 was rebodied by Harkness Motor Works in 1949, shortly after this picture was taken. *W. A. Camwell*

BELFAST TRAMS SINCE 1945

Above 'Rebuild' 256 has just crossed the Queen's Bridge and is about to turn left from Bridge End into Station Street, heading for the BCDR station on 13 May 1950; the conductor is indicating his intention to the following traffic in the time-honoured way. As road vehicles could only overtake a moving tramcar on the inside, signalling left-hand turns was absolutely critical.

The trolleybus is bound for Knock Road (a short working of the Dundonald route). The tram and trolleybus overhead wires are being 'fed' at this point as indicated by the substantial metal cabinets beside the traction pole and the dark band painted on the pole itself.

The Bedford lorry belongs to the UTA, which, apart from the Belfast area, had a near monopoly of passenger and goods traffic in the Province. The car the left of the picture is an Austin. *H. C. Casserley*

Below 252, seen here in Bridge End, was one of the 41 cars built by the BCT during the period prior to 1913, and rebuilt in 1928-9.

The entire row of shops on the left of the picture has disappeared and the railway bridge in the far background has been replaced by a modern structure capable of taking double track.

When this photograph was taken in August 1950 carts pulled by humans and horses were very common in Belfast - indeed, this particular horse and cart belonged to the Ulster Transport Authority (UTA). The car registered MZ 8458 is a Hillman Minx and is closely followed by a Stewarts Cash Stores Ford 10 cwt van, while the nose of a Morris Commercial is just peeping out of Rotterdam Street on the right.

Many important junctions were controlled by traffic lights activated by vehicles passing over special pads inserted into the roadway. Trams of course could not operate these pads, so special contactors were placed in the overhead line, and one of these is clearly seen here just ahead of 252. One of the 1930s telephone kiosks is seen behind the first traction pole on the right. *Roy Brook*

This photograph of 'Rebuild' 35 taken in 1952 shows it coming down Bridge End preparatory to turning right into Station Street. It will go to the terminus at Queen's Road, reverse, and leaving Station Street again, turn right and make for Ardoyne depot or possibly Ligoniel. 35 is followed by 'Rebuild' 164, as mentioned earlier the first of the class to be 'outshopped' after refurbishing in 1928.

A 'gantry'-style trolleybus overhead has been erected, which allows further use to be made of the tram traction poles. The railway bridge carried the link line between the Great Northern and County Down railways, but was only used for special workings. It was later removed, but in the more enlightened times of the 1980s was reinstated as part of the new Belfast Central rail project.

The advertisements for Smithwick's, Guinness and Gallaher's Condor tobacco are still very relevant today. *Roy Brook*

The same view (or as near as I could safely get) taken in January 1994 shows the degree to which the area has changed. Bridge End is now one-way towards Queen's Bridge, and the far end, leading to the Newtownards Road, is completely unrecognisable compared with the 1952 photo. The building immediately before the new railway bridge (now part of Gibson & Leeper's lawnmower showroom) is about the only building to survive from the previous photograph. *Mike Maybin*

Daimler 240 (GZ 3989) obscures this September 1953 view of 289 at Bridge End, looking towards Short Strand. By this date the out-of-town overhead tram wire had been removed, partly because trams described an anti-clockwise loop (to Mountpottinger Depot via Victoria Street, Cromac Square, East Bridge Street, Albert Bridge, and Albertbridge Road, and from the depot via Albertbridge Road, Newtownards Road, Bridge End and Station Street), and partly to reduce the complication of tram and trolleybus wiring at this junction - particularly after Short Strand Depot opened. 240 has had the 'small route number box' treatment.

The 'Fast Taxi' sign on the building on the left is perhaps an early indication of the increased competition ahead for public transport. All the buildings in the picture have been razed and Bridge End is now one-way in the direction of the City Centre. *A. D. Packer*

BELFAST TRAMS SINCE 1945

Above Chamberlain 346 nears the Ropeworks end of the Newtownards Road in August 1952, heading towards Queen's Road from Mountpottinger Depot. The bridge over the road just discernible in the background belonged to the Belfast & County Down Railway and carried that company's main line to Donaghadee, Ballynahinch and Newcastle. The line was closed a few years before this photograph was taken and the bridge, known for very many years as 'Holywood Arches', was demolished some years later.

The majority of the buildings on the left are still there, though changed in ownership. Although the group of houses near the tram is now all shops, the area is still quite recognisable. *Roy Brook*

Below Returning to Mountpottinger Depot in the early 1950s, 'Rebuild' 22 is on East Bridge Street following a Cregagh-bound trolleybus. On the left of the picture a UTA bus stop sign is attached to a traction pole, while a painted sign proclaims the uncontroversial slogan 'GOD IS LOVE'. Stewart Street, from which the saloon car is emerging in the foreground, led to Haymarket, the main trolleybus depot. In later years there was a very complex network of overhead wires in Stewart Street, Turnley Street and Annette Street, which between them formed the entrances and exits to the depot. The entire area has since been demolished and replaced by modern housing. *A. D. Packer*

Above In addition to water cars, snow ploughs, etc, Belfast possessed a stores car, which bore the fleet number 8. Built in 1931, it is seen here in East Bridge Street in 1950 just passing the Turnley Street entrance to Haymarket trolleybus depot with a McCreary tram, a UTA double-decker bus and three trolleybuses in the background, the nearest of which is returning to the City Hall from Cregagh. MZ 5159, behind No 8, is a Ford 10 cwt van.

No 8's provenance has been difficult to prove. One theory is that H. M. S. Catherwood, a Belfast firm that built a number of bus bodies for the Corporation, constructed the van body on the chassis of Standard Red No 8. However, I believe that it is more likely that the body was built by the Corporation on a 5 ft 6 in wheelbase truck and took the fleet number following the retirement of Standard Red No 8 in 1930. There is general agreement, however, that the van entered service on 25 May 1931.

This area has been totally redeveloped into modern two- and three-storey houses and is unrecognisable today. The Central Station and Maysfield leisure centre have been built on the site of the old abattoir just behind the camera. *R. C. Ludgate*

Left McCreary 437 was on the railway bridge in East Bridge Street when photographed in August 1952. It is just passing under the insulator marking the break between electrical sections (which also applied to trolleybuses). The switch box, clearly seen on the 'into-town' side, is painted white for the benefit of drivers and motormen.

'Rebuild' 254, a trolleybus, a BCT double- and single-decker and a UTA single-decker can be seen in the background. The BCT single-decker carries the route number 76 and is presumably heading for Cherryvalley, Gilnahirk or Mann's Corner, all of which used this route number!

The Electricity Department's massive power station - built in about 1905 partly in response to the additional current required by the electric trams - has today been demolished in its entirety. *Roy Brook*

BELFAST TRAMS SINCE 1945

Above 'Rebuild' 255 is heading from Mountpottinger Depot along Albertbridge Road towards Newtownards Road and thence to Queen's Road for the evening exodus from the shipyard, preceded by another rebuild and a Chamberlain, both unidentified. The Albert Wine Lodge on the left is now a bookmaker's shop, while the red-brick wall to the right marked the boundary of what was reputedly the largest ropeworks in the world, but which nowadays is an industrial estate. The photograph was probably taken in the early 1950s judging by the layout of the overhead traction wires.

Here is another example of traction poles being painted to signify something special - in this case a 'STOP' sign. Other specially marked poles indicated, for example, insulators in the overhead wire, feeder boxes, overhead line contactors for traffic lights and automatic points in the track. *A. D. Packer*

Below This view of 'Rebuild' 31 was taken in August 1952. The car (which is still fully lined out) has just come out of Mountpottinger Depot, turned up Albertbridge Road and is turning left at the same junction into Newtownards Road. 31 is heading towards Queen's Road, while a trolleybus on the Holywood Road route is just visible in the background. The box on the nearest traction pole indicates the setting of the trolleybus overhead - in this case it is set for the Upper Newtownards Road. By 1952 there was no tramcar overhead beyond this point.

The van just in front of the trolleybus is a battery-powered bread cart owned by Windsor bakery. The bakery itself is no longer, while home-delivered bread and battery-operated vehicles are rare these days. The car on the left, PZ 411, is an Austin. *Roy Brook*

Until recently it was thought that very few colour photographs existed of Belfast trams, the two main groups being Jack Wyse's Electrail slides and Roy Brook's collection, marketed by Leeds Transport Historical Society. However, a further collection, whose copyright is owned by Colour-Rail, has come to light and I have reproduced four of the best ones here.

Above Although it is not possible accurately to date this photograph, it was probably taken in the early 1950s and shows 'Rebuild' 282 laden with shipyard workers heading home to the Shankill Road. Unusually for this period, 282 is still fully lined out. The blue 'STAGE' sign can be seen on the left-hand traction pole.

With the exception of the red-brick building behind the second 'Rebuild', none of the buildings in the photograph is still standing - there is a road flyover at this point and a new railway bridge has just been constructed to link the line out of the Yorkgate (formerly York Road) station with the rest of the Northern Ireland Railways system. *Roy Brook/Leeds Transport Historical Society*

Above McCreary 413 stands at Ballygomartin terminus in 1951 or 1952, just about to leave for a cross-town trip to Balmoral via Bedford Street. The lighter shade of blue on the roof can be seen here, although rusty stains have begun to be very noticeable on the front, rather spoiling the appearance. *Roy Brook/Leeds Transport Historical Society*

Left Chamberlain 350 slowly grinds its way up Ligoniel hill with a surprising lack of traffic, even for 1953 when this photograph was taken. Virtually all the houses in this photograph have been demolished to make way for modern dwelling units. *W. G. Robertson/Colour-Rail*

BELFAST TRAMS SINCE 1945

Right Photographed in Donegall Square North, Chamberlain 364 appears to be heading to Queen's Road, although it is possible that the blind has not been changed.

An 'ALIGHTING STOP' can just be seen to the left of the tram and two trolleybuses are about to depart for Castlereagh and (possibly) Cregagh, while the one coming up Chichester Street towards the camera is returning from Holywood Road. Lasting less than six years, this was the record-holder for the shortest-lived trolleybus route in Belfast. Its untimely closure was brought about, in part, by the construction of the Sydenham By-Pass and its junction with Holywood Road.

The large red four-storied sandstone building - known to most Belfast people as the 'Water Office' - was built by Lanyon, Lynn and Lanyon as a ware-house for Richardson Sons & Owden between 1867 and 1869. It was taken over by the Water Commissioners after the War and was bought - and tasteful-ly restored - by Marks & Spencer. The taxi beside the Water Office (just under the 'NO WAITING' sign) is an Austin and it is followed by a Vauxhall. The small black car sandwiched between the two trolleybuses is also an Austin.
W. G. Robertson/Colour-Rail

Centre right A typical view of downtown Belfast in the early 1950s. Chamberlain 376 has just left the traffic island in Donegall Square North *en route* to the crossover in College Square East. The dark blue of the tram - officially known as Princess blue - con-trasts with the red of the buses.

In 1905 all trams were painted red and this lasted until 1928 when William Chamberlain wanted to upgrade the Transport Department's image and chose to alter the livery from red to blue. However, only modernised trams and buses were so treated and the perception arose whereby red was old and blue was new.

However, it was later found that the red paint lasted longer than the blue, and from the late 1940s onwards all new vehicles were delivered in red. Trams, being destined for abandonment, were not repainted in the new colour, and the perception altered to red being new and blue being old! The few Standard Reds remaining suddenly became the 'right' colour by reason of being left behind the last time around!
W. G. Robertson/Colour-Rail

Right McCreary 440 is about to depart from College Square East for Ligoniel in 1953. Once the main cross-town routes to South Belfast had been converted to bus operation, the Ligoniel service was diverted to a new crossover in College Square East, where the stationary cars caused little disruption to traffic.

A Corporation bus is barely visible behind the tram - this street did not become one-way until 1958 - and a deliv-ery bike (or message-bike as it was often called) is also present, something rarely seen nowadays.

Although the Mayfair cinema has been replaced by a modern office block, the fab-ric of the old buildings between it and Wellington Place is pretty well intact. The Mayfair cinema was originally known as the Kelvin after the famous Lord Kelvin (inventor of the Atlantic cable, Thompson's compass, the absolute temperature scale and the electricity meter) who is reputed to have lived in a house on this site in the 18th century. *W. G. Robertson/Colour-Rail*

Above The next series of photographs was taken in and around Mountpottinger Depot. Until a few weeks before the complete abandonment of trams in Belfast, there were two main operational depots - Ardoyne and Mountpottinger. The latter provided many of the rush-hour cars for the Queen's Road route, but because the track on Mountpottinger Road itself was abandoned before the war, access to and from the depot was rather tortuous.

Given that the trolleybus overhead was also quite complicated at this busy junction, at certain places trams abandoned their own wires and joined the trolleybus overhead for short periods! A further complication was that additional trolleybus curves were put in to facilitate depot workings as can be seen in this view of McCreary 407 on Albertbridge Road and a sister on Mountpottinger Road; 407 is about to return to the Ballygomartin Road, with its trolley on the trolleybus wire. The depot is out of sight down the road to the left, and the road barely visible to the right is Castlereagh Street where the crossover was.

The trolleybus curves from Albertbridge Road into Castlereagh Street were used only for Castlereagh trolleybuses working to and from Haymarket depot. This junction is barely recognisable today. *Roy Brook*

Below The former Picturedrome cinema (then showing *Les Miserables* with Michael Rennie and Robert Newton) provides the background to 'Rebuild' 265 about to turn right into the depot in September 1953. In the distance can be seen two trolleybuses and another tram about to reverse over the crossover in Castlereagh Street before heading for the depot. The complex web of overhead wires necessary for this junction is also visible at the extreme right of the picture.

The cinema and all the buildings on the left as far as the junction indicated by the striped traffic light poles were demolished some time ago to make way for a major road junction and new housing. *A. D. Packer*

Right 405 has just emerged from Mountpottinger Depot and is about to head towards Queen's Road to pick up the workers there.

This photograph gives a very good idea of the complex web of tram and trolleybus overhead wires at this junction. In order to reduce the sheer weight of overhead wires and fittings, it was arranged at some complex junctions for trams to use the positive trolleybus wire (this was always the wire furthest from the footpath). 405 is about to turn left, while the normal route for trolleybuses here was straight on. Therefore there was a 'frog' (overhead point) operated by means of wires and pulleys leading to a handle on a convenient traction pole.

The oncoming Chamberlain is also on the trolleybus overhead, but after crossing the junction it will regain a 'tram only' wire before running right into the depot. *Roy Brook*

Left Trams continued to be based at Mountpottinger Depot long after most East Belfast routes had been converted to trolleybus or motorbus operation. The picture was taken in June 1948 in Castlereagh Street looking towards Mountpottinger Road and the City Centre; car 90 is standing on the crossover preparatory to crossing Mountpottinger junction and making for the depot. *John H. Meredith*

Right About to cross Albertbridge Road from Castlereagh Street, Chamberlain 382 was heading back to Mountpottinger Depot when photographed by R. J. S. Wiseman in June 1953. The handle attached to the nearest traction pole was to allow the trolleybus driver to determine in which direction the trolleys would travel at the junction in the overhead wires. In this case the mechanism was automatically reset after use - the wording on the poles read 'PULL & LET GO'. Some less frequently used junctions were arranged so that the conductor needed to retain pressure on the handle until the manoeuvre was complete. The wording in such cases read 'PULL & HOLD'. *R. J. S. Wiseman*

Above McCreary 395, one of those built locally by the Service Motor Works, is returning to Mountpottinger Depot heading an interesting line-up of public transport vehicles in Albertbridge Road. It is about to turn right into Castlereagh Street - the position of the trolley pole on the right-hand pair of trolleybus wires confirms this.

Immediately behind and to the inside of the tram is a UTA single-decker bus (possibly a Leyland PS1), an Austin delivery van, an unidentified Chamberlain also bound for Mountpottinger, a trolleybus heading for Dundonald via Albert Bridge judging from the route number, and (just!) a BCT post-war Daimler returning to the City Hall from Sydenham. *R. J. S. Wiseman*

Below Photographed on the last day of tramcar operation on the Bloomfield route is Standard Red 178, seen at the terminus. Evidence of the trolleybus overhead is visible, which has been constructed using the gantry method (ie attaching a piece of tubular steel between the tram traction poles), allowing them to be used for a further period, but supporting the much heavier trolleybus overhead. In fact, trams actually used the 'live' trolleybus overhead wire for part of the route. The branching frog used where the routes of tram and trolleybus diverge can clearly be seen in this photograph. The semi-detached houses have changed very little since this picture was taken. *D. G. Coakham*

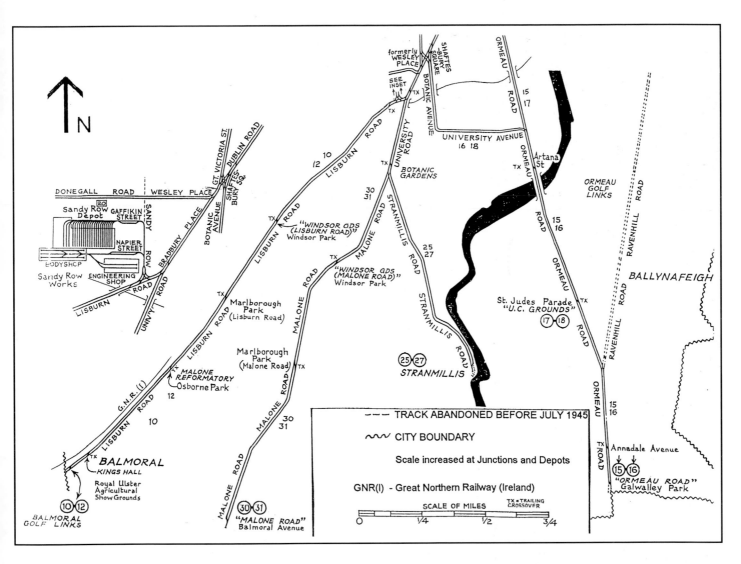

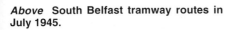

THIS section includes the routes to Ormeau Road, Stranmillis Road, Malone Road, and Great Victoria Street, University Road, and Lisburn Road to Balmoral. The only South Belfast route to have been abandoned was Ravenhill Road, which had gone over to bus operation in 1940.

Above South Belfast tramway routes in July 1945.

Right Standard Red 153 was on a short working on the Ormeau Road at the UC Grounds crossover in Ormeau Road when photographed on 3 October 1946. The bus alongside is an unidentified Bedford OWB of Belfast Corporation. During the war many undertakings, including Belfast, were supplied with utility buses; though adequate for short journeys, they were manufactured to a very basic specification, including wooden

seats. Although trolleybuses did not replace trams on this route until 1948, the overhead was already in place by the time this photograph was taken.

The red-brick building in the background is the local telephone exchange. It is still there, though with considerable anti-terrorist protection. D. G. Coakham

Left There was a short period between February and April 1948 when both buses and trams served Ormeau Road, although the buses went a little bit further up the road to a turning circle called 'Fortbreda' - a term not in widespread public use and never shown on destination screens. The BCT 'BUS STOP' sign is just visible to the left of the picture, while an NIRTB sign can be seen on the out-of-town side.

The photograph was taken on 6 April 1948 and shows Moffetts 333, 331 and 310 at the terminus near Knockbreda Park. The terminus was initially a few hundred yards further up the Ormeau Road, but had been cut back by the time this photograph was taken. The 'trailing' point on the 'into town' track has also been removed to save unnecessary maintenance.

Although the area generally remains recognisable, today the street lighting has been upgraded; the double-fronted house to the right has been converted into flats and the front garden has become a car park. *D. G. Coakham*

Right Built in 1935 as part of the batch of 50 new cars named after the then General Manager, Major McCreary, 423 was on the Stranmillis Road heading into town when this photograph was taken in June 1948. At that time the Stranmillis route was linked with the BNCR Station at York Road, and the destination displayed was 'LMS RLY NCC' - London, Midland & Scottish Railway (Northern Counties Committee). This reflected the various railway amalgamations on the mainland, by which the BNCR became, by turn, first part of the Midland Railway, then the LMS. The Northern Ireland part of the latter group, formed in 1923, was administered by a committee known as, not surprisingly, the LMS Railway (Northern Counties Committee).

The estate behind the stone wall was soon to become Stranmillis Training College for teachers. *John H. Meredith*

Left This view of Stranmillis terminus looking countrywards with the River Lagan on the left is rather unusual - more often the camera was pointed towards the City Centre. Seen in the late 1940s, Moffett 327 has reversed over the terminal stub and is ready to return to Crumlin Road via Castle Junction - or rather, it will when the conductor returns!

Although this area of the city was still gas-lit at this time, each tram terminus was electrically illuminated from the traction supply. The area on the other side of the river has now been built up rather and a safety fence has been erected just behind the tram, but otherwise the scene has not changed that much. *A. D. Packer*

Chamberlain 347 has just arrived from 'LMS Railway' when this view was taken in June 1948. When buses replaced trams on this route in July 1951 the short portion of route between Stranmillis Road and the terminus at Harleston Street was always very poorly patronised and was finally abandoned altogether in the early 1970s. At this time gas lighting was still used in this part of Belfast and there is no evidence yet of private cars. *John H. Meredith*

164 was the first car to be rebuilt out of the batch of 50 in 1929-9, and is seen here on a wintry day at Stranmillis terminus having just had its trolley turned in preparation for the return trip to 'N C RY'. The 'via' blind in the centre window of the lower saloon reads 'VIA GT. VICTORIA ST. & PASSES G. N. RLY'. The tram is beautifully lined out, spotlessly clean and the picture was posed for the *Belfast Telegraph* to publicise the 'new' blue cars. *Belfast Telegraph*

Above McCreary 397, one of the batch built by Service Motor Works in 1935, was on the Malone Road-Ballygomartin route when photographed at Botanic Gardens in July 1951, looking down University Road towards the City Centre.

The concrete telephone kiosk and a street fire alarm can be seen on the right of the picture, while the buildings to the left have all since been replaced with a modern block. The lorry is a Scammell 'mechanical horse' and trailer and both it and the horse and trap beside it are very much things of the past. *R. C. Jackson*

Below This photograph was taken in May 1994 and shows that considerable changes have taken place over the last 40-odd years. On the left the three-storey terrace has given way to a plain brick office block owned by the Ulster Bank, while on the right the telephone kiosk, public fire alarm and the gate lodge to Botanic Gardens have all disappeared. There has also sprouted a plethora of traffic signs that no doubt contribute to road safety, but do little to enhance the visual appeal of the junction. *Mike Maybin*

Right Chamberlain 384 is seen at Malone terminus in 1951, with the camera pointing towards the 'end of the lines', as the terminus was often called in Belfast. This is a further example of an intention to extend the track that was never carried out, and eventually the track on the right was severed from the crossover to reduce wear.

Today the road has since been greatly widened and Balmoral Avenue (where the nearest car is) has become a major junction. The little gate lodge to the right still protects the entrance to Malone Park; this is one of the very few private roads left in Belfast and as such the owners are allowed to close it at the Lisburn Road end. The large clump of trees in the centre of the photograph marks what is now an exclusive residential development (as the estate agents would say). *H. B. Priestley*

Left Another view of Malone terminus, this time looking towards the City Centre; Moffett 330 is just about to cross to the other track before its return journey. The precise date of the photograph is not known, but judging from the white-painted bumpers, wastepaper bin and striped traction poles in the distance, I would say that it was taken shortly after the end of the War. Today the buildings are unchanged from the photograph. *C. Carter*

Right The final photograph at Malone terminus was taken by A. R. Spencer in 1947 and shows 'Rebuild' 31 about to return to Ballygomartin. This is a further example of the majority of the 'Rebuild' batch that retained side windows deeper than those at the ends, giving, in my view, a rather ungainly appearance. *A. R. Spencer*

BELFAST TRAMS SINCE 1945

Above Showing a scruffy appearance that was not characteristic, Moffett 297 was in Great Victoria Street *en route* from Shankill Road to Malone Road when A. D. Packer took this view, probably in the very early 1950s. Most trams in Belfast carried 'via' boards held on brackets at the bottom of the rear window, and this one indicates 'VIA SHANKILL ROAD & GT. VICTORIA ST'.

A battery-operated bread cart belonging to the former Windsor bakery can just be seen in the distance. Although the street scene has changed greatly today, the Crown liquor saloon seen here between the tram and the Singer car has been preserved by the National Trust. Even so, it still sells real beer! *A. D. Packer*

Below Seen here at 2.20 pm (if the station clock is to be believed) on an August day in 1952 is McCreary 428 outside the terminus of the Great Northern Railway of Ireland in Great Victoria Street, from which trains left for the south and west of the Province. Most unfortunately this magnificent terminus was demolished about 1970 to make way for the Europa Hotel. However, as the main line to Dublin crossed the International Frontier, the GNR(I) was exempt for some years from the 1948 Nationalisation scheme that applied to most of the other railways in Northern Ireland.

The tram is bound for Marlborough Park, a short working of the Balmoral route. The few cars that worked to Marlborough Park tended not to display route numbers.

The car on the left, FZ 5542, is a pre-war Austin, while that on the right, OZ 8211, is a Hillman Minx. A Ford and another Austin can just be seen parked in the station forecourt. *Roy Brook*

Right Although the location of this photograph is probably instantly recognisable to anyone who has travelled by bus or tram to see the famous 'Blues' (Linfield) play football at Windsor Park, nearly all the buildings in the photograph have since been replaced. However, their successors are in sympathy with the general proportions of the area and thankfully do not include tower blocks.

Moffett 307 is heading along Lisburn Road towards Balmoral in August 1952, closely followed by a Guy lorry owned by James McVeigh & Sons. Sandy Row - the street off to the left - was the location of the Tramways Department's main depot and works. The tram itself carries a spare route board just visible to the right of the driver, the wording on which reads 'VIA CRUMLIN ROAD'. *R. J. S. Wiseman*

Centre right The junction of Lisburn Road with University Road is still recognisable in 1994, but there have been great changes since Richard Wiseman took the previous photograph. The buildings at the corner of Sandy Row have been replaced by a tastefully designed block of four-storey brick shops and dwellings, and the row of shops on University Road itself has also been extensively altered. *Mike Maybin*

Left Although the destination reads 'MARLB PARK LISBURN ROAD', Standard red 153 is passing Tate's Avenue on Lisburn Road heading towards the City Centre. By June 1948, when this view was taken, the tram was rather the worse for wear.

Although Belfast had generated electricity for many years, it continued to light the streets by gas into the 1950s, as can be seen by the once elegant gas lamp attached to the section pole on the right!

The Northern Bank at the corner has been substantially rebuilt since this photograph was taken. *John H. Meredith*

Left Even after the main service to Balmoral was provided by buses, a limited number of trams worked to Windsor Grounds, particularly during the rush-hour. Photographed by Bill Haynes in the early 1950s, Standard Red 17 is really looking rather sorry for itself here, about to return to the City Centre from such a Windsor Grounds short working.

Most unusually 17 retains the 'black on white' route number blind. First introduced in the early 1920s, they had virtually all been replaced by the 'white on black' version before the War. *W. J. Haynes*

Right This photograph was taken about 1948 and shows 'Rebuild' 259 on the Lisburn Road on a short working to Windsor Grounds. The conductor is in the process of turning the trolley for the return journey to Bellevue, a short working of the Glengormley route. Although this crossover is often referred to as 'WINDSOR GROUNDS', it should more accurately be called Windsor Park, as it was just north of that junction with Lisburn Road.

The buildings in the background have not changed beyond recognition even today. *R. C. Ludgate*

Left One car, 35, a 'Rebuild' with 'same height' top-deck windows, is having its trolley turned preparatory to its cross-town journey to Shankill Road. It is followed by an unidentified 'Rebuild' and McCreary 402, which will be travelling to Greencastle in North Belfast; a further car is just visible to the right. A scene such as this with four tramcars parked in the middle of one of the busiest roads in Belfast will, regretfully, be unlikely to happen again.

The waste ground to the left was developed into a bus turning circle in the early 1950s, and a little further up the road a filling station was built at about the same time, but otherwise the location would be easily identifiable today. *Burrows Collection, London Borough of Newham Leisure Services*

BELFAST TRAMS SINCE 1945

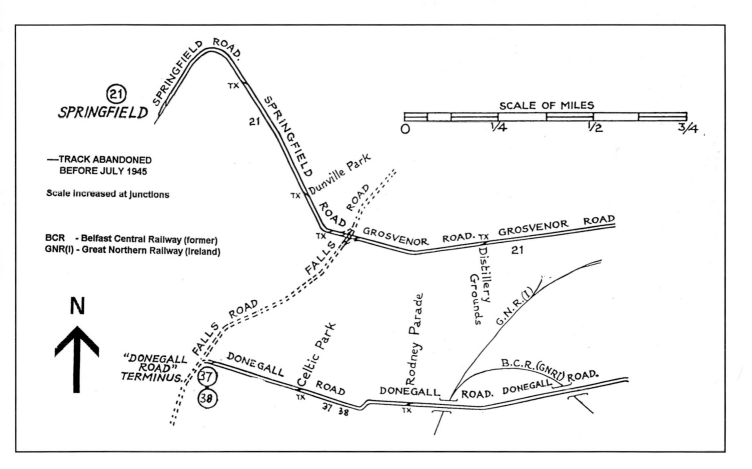

Above **West Belfast tramway routes in July 1945.**

THE ROUTES in West Belfast on which trams still operated after 1945 were Donegall Road, Grosvenor Road and Springfield Road. The main artery in this sector of the city is the Falls Road, whose trams were the first to go in 1938. The experimental trolleybuses that replaced them were so successful that the Corporation decided to convert the whole city over five years.

Above **West Belfast tramway routes in July 1945.**

Right A shot of Standard Red 14 taken on 1 July 1939, together with an unidentified 'Rebuild' on the Donegall Road at Utility Street, which was later to become the Headquarters of the Belfast Corporation Transport Department after the undertaking outgrew Sandy Row in the early 1950s. However, the two cars are probably on a Sunday School outing judging from the mothers and children on the cars and about to board them.

The red-brick building to the left is the Donegall Road library, which is still very much in business today. Although this view was taken some years before the period covered by this book, it is included mainly because the area was unchanged for many years and this photograph could have been taken at any time before the Donegall Road trams were abandoned in 1949. **The receding car is an Austin.** *W. A. Camwell*

Above 284, one of the later cars built by the BCT in its own works in Sandy Row between 1908 and 1913 and rebuilt about 1929, stands at Donegall Road terminus about to have its trolley turned before moving back over the crossover towards the City Centre, the direction in which we are looking.

The out-of-town track originally curved round to the Falls Road to allow access to Falls depot, but that route and depot were converted to trolleybus operation in 1938 and the connecting track lifted shortly thereafter.

The advertisement on the tram for Powell's jams refers to a product now no longer available, but Scribons Kemp still make biscuits in their factory near Grimsby for various supermarket chains who sale them as 'own brand'. *D. G. Coakham*

Above Moffett 332 pauses at Donegall Road terminus in April 1947 a few days before the tramcar service gave way to buses. This particular tram was to last a further six years to give a total of 32 years in service, a record of which many buses today would be incapable - London Routemasters excepted!

The shops on the front of the Falls Road visible to the left and right of the tram are still there, albeit superficially modernised. The air raid shelters along the middle of Rockville Street on the far side of the Falls Road are obviously a legacy of the War, while the street fire alarm disappeared from Belfast, partly for reasons of vandalism and the ease of making false calls, but primarily as a result of the widely available telephone. A major problem of the street alarm system was that the fire brigade had to report to the alarm point before being able to proceed to the fire itself. *D. G. Coakham*

Left This scene in Grosvenor Road would be almost unrecognisable today. The buildings on both sides of the road have all been swept away and replaced by modern red-brick housing, a few shops and the West Link junction and roundabout. The Venus pub on the left was at the corner of Granville Street. The telephone wires on tall poles have been long since replaced by underground cables and the (then) modern electric street lights would now be considered most old-fashioned.

Chamberlain 368 is making its way along Grosvenor Road on its way to Springfield terminus in August 1952. The car parked beside the tram stop - where it should not be - is a Vauxhall. *R. J. S. Wiseman*

BELFAST TRAMS SINCE 1945

Right Chamberlain 344, bound for Shankill Road, stands on Grosvenor Road near Drew Memorial Church in 1952. The area has been extensively redeveloped and, apart from the church, would be unrecognisable today. The houses and shops on the left have been replaced by modern units of one and two storeys. *R. J. S. Wiseman*

Left Fully lined-out Chamberlain 343 prepares to leave Springfield terminus for Shankill Road in July 1951, while McCreary 428 has just arrived. The Chamberlain is fitted with a destination box in the lower saloon as well as route board brackets at the bottom of the rear window, but neither was being used when this photograph was taken. The advertisements carried by the cars for Christie's wallpaper and Player's cigarettes are both for products still available today. *R. C. Jackson*

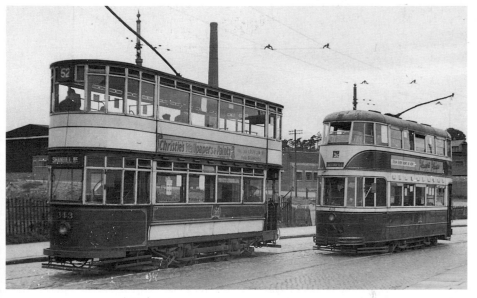

Right Posed at Springfield terminus on 25 May 1952, McCreary 401 is about to begin the return journey to Crumlin Road. The low position of the headlights confirm that the car was built by Service Motor Works. 'Rebuild' 164 already has its trolley turned in readiness for the journey into town, and is about to use the crossover just below the terminus.

Springfield was unusual in having two crossovers at the terminus, which of course facilitated changing the order in which cars departed. The blue 'STAGE' sign is clearly seen, as is the clock mounted on the same traction pole. *H. M. Rea*

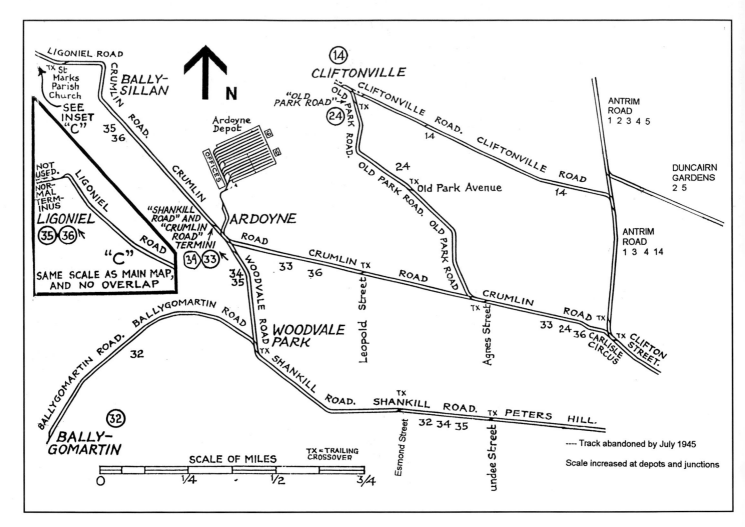

LIGONIEL ROAD
TX St Marks Parish Church
SEE INSET "C"
BALLY-SILLAN
CRUMLIN ROAD
35 36
CRUMLIN ROAD
NOT USED. NORMAL TERMINUS
LIGONIEL ROAD
LIGONIEL
(35) (36)
"SHANKILL ROAD" AND "CRUMLIN ROAD" TERMINI
(34) (33)
"C" SAME SCALE AS MAIN MAP, AND NO OVERLAP

N

Ardoyne Depot
OFFICES
6 6
ARDOYNE ROAD
34 35
WOODVALE ROAD
33 36
WOODVALE PARK
TX SHANKILL ROAD.

(14) CLIFTONVILLE
"OLD PARK ROAD"
OLD PARK ROAD
(24)
CLIFTONVILLE ROAD.
14
CLIFTONVILLE ROAD
24
TX Old Park Avenue
14
OLD PARK ROAD. OLD PARK ROAD
CRUMLIN TX ROAD
Leopold Street
Agnes Street
TX
CRUMLIN ROAD TX
33 24 36 CARLISLE CIRCUS
TX CLIFTON STREET.

ANTRIM ROAD 1 2 3 4 5
DUNCAIRN GARDENS 2 5
ANTRIM ROAD 1 3 4 14

BALLYGOMARTIN ROAD. BALLYGOMARTIN ROAD
32
(32) BALLY-GOMARTIN

SHANKILL ROAD. TX SHANKILL ROAD. TX PETERS HILL.
32 34 35
Esmond Street
undee Street

SCALE OF MILES
TX = TRAILING CROSSOVER
0   1/4   1/2   3/4

---- Track abandoned by July 1945
Scale increased at depots and junctions

THIS area includes the routes to Ballygomartin, Shankill, Crumlin Road, Ligoniel, Oldpark and Cliftonville Road. Virtually no tram routes had been abandoned in this area by the end of the war; in fact, the Ligoniel route was the last to be converted to buses in 1954.

Above **North West Belfast tramway routes in July 1945.**

Left **Moffett 330 is bound for the Queen's Road, passing St Matthew's Church of Ireland on Shankill Road at the corner of Cambrai Street in 1952. This street marks the division between the Shankill Road proper and Woodvale Road.**
Although the lower Shankill Road has undergone a great deal of redevelopment, and not all of it for the better, this area is still easily recognisable. *R. J. S. Wiseman*

Above Proceeding towards the crossover in College Square East, notwithstanding the destination blind being set at 'CITY HALL', Chamberlain 370 is just passing Hartington Bar on the Shankill Road. McCreary 432 is going in the opposite direction and can be identified as one of the 20 McCrearys built by English Electric because of its headlamps being in the high position.

The flags and bunting on the shops are in honour of the Coronation, and the photograph was taken from Moffett 340 on the occasion of a special LRTL tour in June 1953. *John Price*

Below In August 1952, at the junction of the Ballygomartin Road and Woodvale Road, outside Woodvale Presbyterian Church,

Moffett 329 is emerging from Ballygomartin Road bound for Balmoral, while Chamberlain 380, heading for Ligoniel, is about to take on some passengers. The box on the traction standard on the left houses the light that indicates that the automatic points have been correctly set. The 'STAGE' sign on the right indicates a fare stage and is not a Board of Trade compulsory stop.

The lone policeman quietly surveying the traffic, which includes a Riley and a Humber (both back view), is a reflection of more peaceful times. We are looking towards the Ligoniel terminus, and the area has hardly changed in the intervening 40 years since the photograph was taken. *Roy Brook*

Above Photographed at the top of the Woodvale Road, Chamberlain 350 is looking very smart considering that only six months remained until the total disappearance of trams from the streets of Belfast. To the left of the photograph there are bus and tram stop signs on the same traction pole in preparation for the changeover on the Crumlin Road, Shankill and Ligoniel routes. The process began on 18 May 1953, and tram journeys were gradually replaced by buses; by October trams were no longer advertised in the public timetable, although rush-hour services continued to operate for some months.

The old-style pedestrian crossing with Belisha beacons but without the 'zebra' stripes on the road surface can be seen, as can the concrete telephone kiosk at the junction of Twaddell Avenue. The little brick building just to the left of the tram was a gents public toilet.

The van in the distance with the round windows in its rear doors to the right of the tram belongs to the mineral water manufacturers Cantrell & Cochrane, and the famous 'C&C' logo embraced the window holes quite neatly. Incidentally, C&C are still very much in business at the time of writing. There is also an advertisement for Gallaher's cigarettes, and that firm is also of course still trading. The general layout of the area has not altered very much today. *Roy Brook*

Below Chamberlain 349 stands at Ballygomartin Road terminus in August 1952. Behind it the square setts are being removed as part of the preparation for the replacement of trams on this route by buses. The word 'square', as applied to the setts in Belfast, is a bit of a misnomer as the setts used were rectangular.

Bound for Balmoral with destination and route number blinds correctly set, 349 is very well turned out for her last year and a half in service. *Roy Brook*

Right Standard Red 120 and McCreary 420 stand at Ballygomartin terminus in June 1948. Although 120 was fitted with 'via' blinds in the centre window of the lower saloon, a 'via' board is also carried tucked under the stairs behind the dash. The fact that the route number is set at blank suggests that the tram was on a special working.

The white wall in the background is part of the bridge over the Forth River. (Scottish readers might be surprised to know that we also have a Forth, albeit rather smaller - ours is only about 4 feet wide!) The traction poles and elegant gas lamp standard have retained their wartime black and white striped bases. *John H. Meredith*

Left Chamberlain 381 is seen at Ballygomartin terminus in the early 1950s with a very youthful motorman at the controls! The (real) motorman has just let down the step ready for the return journey to Malone Road and presumably is about to turn the trolley. The fact that no route number is shown suggests that this was a rush-hour working.

The school in the background - Forth River Primary - is very much still in business although protected by a more modern warning sign! Indeed, the general physical surroundings have changed little in the intervening period since the photograph was taken. *I. R. Davidson*

Right Chamberlain 349 stands with an unidentified 'Rebuild' at Ballygomartin terminus in August 1952. At this stage there were still some cross-town routes operating, one of which was Ballygomartin-Malone Road. Although bound for Malone, 349 has not yet had the blinds changed in preparation for the return trip.

The little cast iron structure surmounted by the gas lamp, barely visible behind the hedge to the right of the tram, is a gents toilet. Although primarily intended for the convenience of tram crews, they were also accessible to the public, and were located at a number of other termini including Ligoniel and Balmoral. All have since been demolished. In the background there is a nice view the mountains that surround Belfast. *Roy Brook*

Above Chamberlain 377 is in Clifton Street, just below Carlisle Circus, in August 1953, and is heading to Ligoniel via Crumlin Road during the last few months of tram operation. The trolleybus overhead wires have been in place for the Glengormley route since 1949, four years before this photograph was taken. Carlisle Circus was unusual in trolleybus operation in that the overhead layout was designed to allow trolleybuses coming from either direction to turn here.

The tram 'STAGE' sign is attached to the traction pole on the right, which also carries the feeders to the overhead. The 'jumper' wires from the trolleybus overhead to the tram wire can clearly be seen. The bus and trolleybus 'STAGE' sign is only just visible behind the tramcar and the temporary RAC sign for the Dundrod circuit has been lashed to a convenient traction pole.

The statue in the middle of Carlisle Circus is of 'Roaring Hugh Hanna', a fundamentalist preacher. It was erected in 1894 and demolished by the IRA in the early days of 'The Troubles'. His church - St Enoch's Presbyterian - has also just been demolished - legitimately! The group of shops to the right, however, remains today, though they have undergone numerous changes of use and ownership in the four decades or so since this photograph was taken. The car heading up Clifton Street with its back to the camera is a Morris 8. *Roy Brook*

Below Although the area is easily recognisable in May 1994 compared with 1953, a number of changes have taken place. St Enoch's Presbyterian Church has been replaced with a much more modest structure.

After lying derelict for many years the pub (formerly known as the Criterion) on the north side of Carlisle Circus is being modernised. In the process, however, it has lost its attic window. *Mike Maybin*

Above McCreary 432 is *en route* for the City Hall at Carlisle Circus in June 1953, looking rather drab. It is followed by another McCreary going to the County Down station. 432 has had the left direction indicator light removed altogether, leaving an unpainted spot on the waistband, while the right-hand one has been plated over. The second McCreary, however, has both lights *in situ*. Both trams were built by English Electric.

The 'lie' of the track on the Antrim Road can just be seen to the right of 432, though this route was converted to trolleybuses in 1949. Note the 'TURN LEFT' sign, which obviously does apply to tramcars!

Behind the second tram a Belfast Corporation Daimler is bound for Harberton Park, a short working of the Balmoral route. It lasted only for a brief period, and was discontinued when the turning circle at King's Hall was completed. The new terminus was shown as 'BALMORAL SHOW GROUNDS' for many years on bus destina-

tion blinds, but Citybus (successor to the Belfast Corporation) has reverted to the much better known 'KING'S HALL'.

This general area was very badly run down in the 1970s, partly as a result of 'The Troubles', but partly also as a result of redevelopment, including the construction of the 'Westlink' road. However, there are welcome signs of a rejuvenation of the area today. *R. J. S. Wiseman*

Below This part of the Crumlin Road was dominated by the Courthouse on the left (out of the photograph) and the jail visible to the right of the tram. Both are still very much there, though with greatly re-inforced security measures. A tunnel under the Crumlin Road very conveniently connects the two establishments! Chamberlain 349 is passing the jail and making for the City Hall. *Roy Brook*

Above McCreary 397 was photographed by Richard Wiseman in June 1953 on the Crumlin Road, heading towards the City Centre. It is *en route* to the City Hall and is passing Ewart's mill on the left and Cambrai Street on the extreme right. This mill and others gave a lot of employment for women in the area, but the work was hard and not well paid.

A Belisha beacon marks a pedestrian crossing place - no black and white stripes on the road yet - while one of the old 'KEEP LEFT' bollards can be seen in the mouth of Cambrai Street. *R. J. S. Wiseman*

Below 434 makes its way down Crumlin Road towards the City Centre with the destination display reading 'AGNES STREET CRUMLIN ROAD', suggesting that the crew have not bothered to change it. The BCT bus in the background is near where the Crumlin Road is joined by Woodvale Road, and is probably on a special working, as a regular bus service on the Crumlin Road was not established until some time after this photograph was taken in 1952.

The old-style pedestrian crossing (controlled by traffic lights rather than Belisha beacons) is evident, with metal studs marking the crossing before the black and white 'zebra' stripes became common. Today rioting and redevelopment have combined to remove virtually all the houses on the right-hand side of the road and replace them with modern dwelling units. *Roy Brook*

Right With the background of the gentle rise of Black Mountain, this photograph of 349 taken in August 1952 shows clearly to the right of the tram the Ardoyne 'Loney' - later officially named 'Road' - and the tracks to Ardoyne tram depot, the newest of Belfast's depots, commissioned in 1913 to house the cars required for the extensions opened in January of that year; this area was to be the site of the future Ardoyne bus garage. In the background the lower slopes have been built up mainly with public and private housing.

Just behind the tram is the waste ground upon which will be built the bus turning circle. To the right of the picture is one of the 'STAGE' signs. Both the flags themselves and the poles on which they were mounted remained around Belfast for very many years after the last tram had gone.

The open lorry parked on the Crumlin Road just beside the Moffett is a Bedford, one of a fleet owned by Coleman's of Glarryford. The one near the shops is a short-wheelbase Fordson tipper owned by P. F. Kerr Ltd. *Roy Brook*

Centre right Just about to go into service to pick up shipyard workers on the Queen's Road in August 1953, 427 is on the double track exit from the depot and is ready to join the 'main line'. The destination display at the side is not very informative - 'SHANKILL ROAD via SHANKILL ROAD' - or perhaps is set for the return journey!

I doubt that the wording of the advertisement on the side of the tram - 'From every point of view PLAYER'S PLEASE' - would find universal support today. The general area is still easily recognisable at the present time, although the lower reaches of the hills are somewhat built up, and the beginning of housing development can be seen by comparison with the previous photograph of 349. The row of little shops on the right is now com-

Right This view was taken outside Ardoyne Depot looking down the Crumlin Road towards the City Centre and shows Moffett 328 and an unidentified McCreary with a couple of other cars in the background. The overhead wire leading into the depot entrance on the left can just be seen.

The Northern Ireland Road Transport Board was just giving way to the Ulster Transport Authority when this photograph was taken in June 1948, but the NIRTB's bus stops are still in place. *John H. Meredith*

Left These three photographs are included to show the relative luxury of the Belfast McCreary cars. Photographed by John Gillham on the Crumlin Road on 13 June 1953, less than a year before the total abandonment of the trams, 423 has been maintained in fairly good condition (apart from the rather obvious dent - or 'dinge' in the local language - in the rear off-side!).

The McCreary cars were introduced in 1935 and the order to build them was split between the English Electric Company and the local firm of Service Motor Works. As already mentioned, the main external methods of distinguishing between the two batches were the position of the headlights and the fleet numbers. The English Electric cars (392 and 423-441) had their headlights in the high position (near the windscreen), while those of the Service cars (393-422) were in the low position (about half-way up the front panel). The cars were fitted with either Crompton-Parkinson or British Thomson-Houston 50 hp traction motors. 392 and 393 had separate driver's cabs, but this was not carried through for the rest of the batch.

There has been a suggestion that the double transverse seats in the lower saloon were replaced by singles on some cars to increase capacity (as was done with some Chamberlains during the war), but a photograph in *Transport World* of 18 July 1935 shows the single seats in place when the cars were new.

The cars were mounted on four-wheel Maley & Taunton trucks - Belfast never operated eight-wheelers - and there were five braking systems, comprising air track brake, air wheel brake, hand wheel brake, rheostat brake and magnetic track brake.

Initially the English Electric cars (ie 392 and most of 423-441) were equipped with illuminated direction indicator arrows, but by the end of the war most had been removed. The McCrearys were also liberally equipped with roller blind destination display indicators. At front and rear there were destination and route number displays, while over each door were destination, 'via' and route number displays.

Centre left The top deck view of 423 taken on the same occasion shows the cushioned blue leather seats, chrome grab rails and handles, modern - for 1935 - ceiling and Art Deco lights, all contributing to the impression of a degree of luxury not previously experienced by Belfast citizens in their public transport vehicles!

Left The lower deck of 423 shows the 'two and one' seating arrangement that allowed for additional standing passengers. The general decor is very much 1930s style and was carried forward into the buses and trolleybuses that were ordered in the period up to the war. *All J. C. Gillham*

BELFAST TRAMS SINCE 1945

Above In many ways this view is typical of a Belfast tramscape, and although it was taken by Roy Brook in August 1952, in fact the scene remained unchanged for very many years; even today it is easily recognisable.

Chamberlain 376 has just turned left from Crumlin Road into Ligoniel Road and is about to climb the hill to Ligoniel village. The small group of shops to the left has changed hands several times of course, and the very small shop or cafe on the right - the Opera - is now a 'Hot Food Take Away', having changed its allegiance from Coca Cola to Pepsi! Small businesses like these provided an invaluable service to their communities - often providing a weekly credit facility for families on low Incomes. *Roy Brook*

Below This view was taken from the same position early in 1994 and shows how the Victorian houses have been successfully refurbished while retaining their essential character. *Mike Maybin*

Above This view of Chamberlain 390 on Ligoniel Road heading down from the village of Ligoniel on its way to Balmoral in 1951 shows off the handsome lines of this type of car extremely well. This part of the route was fairly prosperous in the early post-war years, as can be seen from the relatively large houses on the right-hand side of the road. The pillars without railings on the left - they were sacrificed for the War Effort some years earlier - mark the boundary of Glenbank Park. The early type of 'flaming torch' school warning sign is just visible in the left distance, and electric street lighting has recently been installed. *W. J. Wyse*

Below *En route* to the City Hall in August 1952, Chamberlain 377 has just left Ligoniel terminus and is descending the very steep hill, which in the days before air-braked trams had a number of compulsory 'Board of Trade' stops. Although these were not always observed after the introduction of air-braked trams, they were probably never officially rescinded. Very few of the buildings in the photograph remain today, and the left-hand side of the road is well built up, mostly with modern two-storey housing. *Roy Brook*

Right This 1951 view of Ligoniel Road with McCreary 407 gives a good idea of the long trek up to Ligoniel terminus. Even in the 'mechanised' 1950s track repairs were largely carried out by hand. The out-of-town tracks have sunk below the level of the square setts and, if not repaired, severe damage could be caused to the trams' motor casings, which were only a few inches above the level of the roadway.

On the left-hand footpath a small boy can be seen pushing a 'soap-box', or, as it is better known in Belfast, a 'guider'. Although a long haul up Ligoniel Hill, the thrill of riding a guider down it must have been something else! *Roy Brook*

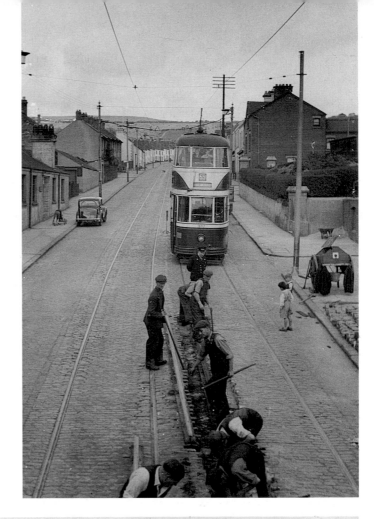

Below This view of Moffett 327, taken on 25 May 1952, with a 'full-frontal' of 'Rebuild' 164 on Ligoniel Road almost at the terminus, captures something of the atmosphere of Ligoniel village in the 1950s. Although it was placed within the Belfast City area in 1896, the village always retained an air of independence. Its people tended to work in the local factory, mill and shops, and it had its own Protestant and Roman Catholic churches and schools.

A good example of a Belfast 'Board of Trade' stop can be seen on the left of the picture. As Ligoniel Road was a very steep hill, these compulsory stops were a necessary passenger safety measure. The signs had 'ALL CARS' on the top border, 'STOP' in the centre in black letters on a white ground, and 'HERE' on the bottom border in white letters on a red ground; they were sometimes known as 'Red' stops. The poles on which they were mounted were also differently painted to emphasise their importance. *H. M. Rea*

Above Chamberlain 383 is about to return to 'CITY HALL' (or more accurately the crossover in College Square East). 383 was one of the ten Chamberlains built locally by Service Motor Works and is followed by an unidentified Moffett and McCreary 406, one of the 'low headlamp' cars also built by Service. When this picture was taken, on 6 June 1953, the Ligoniel route was linked across the City Centre to the BCDR station (shown on some destination screens as 'C. DOWN RLY.').

Both Crosse & Blackwell's soups and Cadbury's chocolate are still going strong, unlike the buildings in the background, all of which have been demolished to make way for more modern housing. *Courtesy David Harvey*

Below Although a programme of fitting top covers to Standard Reds and ex-horse cars was begun in 1908, for some reason 244-250 inclusive were not so treated and remained open topped until the end of their days. The precise date of this photograph is not known but it is certainly pre-1947 and, judging from the dress of the men, possibly earlier. The destination 'CRUMLIN ROAD' on both front and side blinds suggests that the car is about to run into Ardoyne depot.

The little stone construction with the gas lamp above in the background is a gents toilet primarily for platform staff but also open to the public. I wonder why in years gone by so many gents toilets were built, yet so very few ladies conveniences? *C. L. Fry*

Above This view shows McCreary 409, with an unidentified Chamberlain very much in the background at Ligoniel terminus in June 1953; the destination reads 'C. DOWN RLY.'. This is a Service Motor Works McCreary, and the side advertisement for Inglis's bread referred to a well-known and long-established Belfast bakery now trading under the national banner of Mother's Pride. All the mill houses to the left have since been demolished. *Courtesy David Harvey*

Below Just in the process of having its trolley turned in preparation for the return trip to Balmoral, Moffett 293 was photographed at Ligoniel by John Meredith in January 1950. The line of the former complex terminal layout is clearly seen in this picture; this was one of the most complex termini in Belfast, most of which had a single trailing crossover. Other examples of more complex layouts were Queen's Road, with three crossovers, and Springfield Road with two. *John H. Meredith*

Left Seen on a very wet day is Moffett 295, making its way almost empty down the Oldpark Road *en route* to Springfield. The front offside has received a bit of a dent. The group of three-storey houses has since been demolished and to date has not been replaced.

It is not possible accurately to date this view, but the route number suggests that it was before February 1951. *Photographer unknown*

Right Taken in the spring of 1951 by Reg Ludgate, this view shows Chamberlain 354 at the Oldpark Road terminus (with the camera pointing out-of-town). Before the change-over from trams to trolleybuses on the Cliftonville Road in 1947, there was a double-track junction between the two routes. However, the introduction of a trolleybus turning circle at Cliftonville Circus, together with the wiring for the extension to Carr's Glen, required the tramcar overhead to be cut back to the position seen in this photograph. Trolleybus enthusiasts will know that the trolleybus frog was hand operated with automatic reset. *R. C. Ludgate*

Right During 1922 one of the Standard Red cars was fitted with a complete top cover. The work was carried out as economically as possible under the direction of Mr Moffett, the General Manager, as one of his last jobs before leaving for Salford in October of that year. The lower deck platforms were not covered in, and one effect of the new bulkheads was to greatly increase the amount of rain falling on the motorman! No further cars were altered in this way and 89 acquired various nicknames, two of the more repeatable being 'Queen Mary' and 'The Henhouse'.

This photograph was taken in July 1946, again looking in the direction of the Cliftonville terminus. Blakely Bros Home Bakery has since changed hands several times, but the area is not greatly changed in character today. *D. G. Coakham*

BELFAST TRAMS SINCE 1945

THE TWO main routes in this section are Antrim Road to Glengormley and Shore Road to Greencastle, the latter including the Northern Counties Railway station in York Street. By 1945 no electric tram routes in North Belfast had been converted to buses or trolleybuses. In the mid-1880s a short piece of horse tram track was abandoned in Great George's Street and replaced by a route to Northern Counties Railway via Corporation Street. For some reason relatively few photographs are known to have been taken in Corporation Street.

Right North Belfast tramway routes in July 1945.

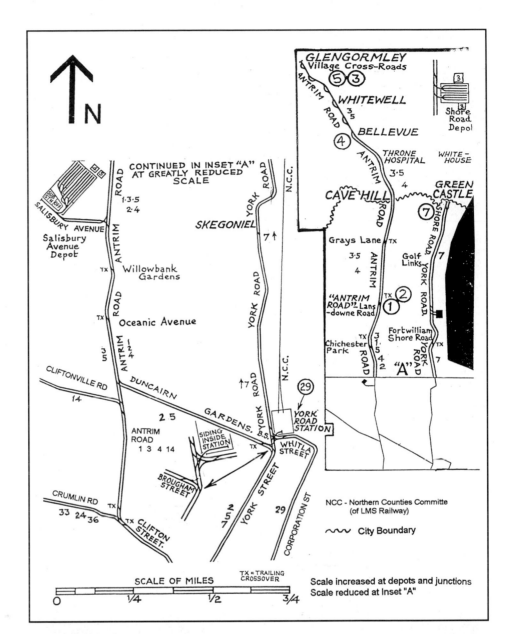

Below right A rather dull January day in 1949 is the setting for this view of Chamberlain 371 on an irregular short working to Gray's Lane on the Antrim Road, looking towards the terminus. When trolleybuses first operated on the Glengormley service the only intermediate turning point was the reversing triangle at Strathmore Park - later upgraded to a turning circle and shown on trolleybus destination blinds as 'ANTRIM ROAD'. I always felt that this was rather unhelpful, given that the Antrim Road was several miles long! However, the very early trolleybus destination blinds featured displays for 'DUNMORE PARK' and 'GRAY'S LANE', although turning facilities were never available at these points.

Gray's Lane was and to a large degree still is a narrow, rural lane running between Antrim Road and Shore Road with neither housing nor footpath for the greater part of its length. *D. G. Coakham*

Above 247 was one of the few ex-horse trams not to receive a top cover. These open-toppers were used regularly on workings to Bellevue, where this shot was taken in the late 1940s. Although the destination screen shows 'CASTLE JN', the car is facing towards Glengormley. The NIRTB bus stop and the blacked-out headlight suggest a date not long after the War, and the fact that both cars are fully lined out would support this.

The Standard Red behind is one of the few to have a 'long top saloon', ie where the top and lower deck saloons were of equal length. The majority of Standards were fitted with top saloons rather shorter than those of the lower deck. *F. N. T. Jones*

Left On the occasion of the replacement of the Glengormley tram service by trolleybuses a group of enthusiasts hired a tramcar for a tour of the system. They chose 238 an ex-horse tram, which was converted to electric traction in 1905, rebuilt and top-covered shortly after and performed sterling duty until its retirement in 1949, by which date it was approaching 50 years of age. Would any reader care to admit to being present in this photograph, which was taken on the Antrim Road on 24 January 1949? *H. M. Rea*

BELFAST TRAMS SINCE 1945

Above Bellevue Zoo on a wet day in June 1948 is the setting for this picture of Chamberlain 368, returning to Castle Junction from a short working to Bellevue. The AA sign to the right of the picture reads 'TO MOTOR PARK' - in fact the zoo car park. Just a little way down the Antrim Road, on the same side, a Northern Ireland Road Transport Board (NIRTB) bus stop peeps crookedly out of the trees. It was in 1948 that the NIRTB was replaced by the Ulster Transport Authority (UTA) in the hope that a more efficient public transport system would emerge. Whether or not this happened is very much a moot point! *John H. Meredith*

Below Photographed by John Meredith in June 1948, 269 is about to depart from Glengormley terminus for Castle Junction. The wording on the 'STOP' signs reads 'ALL CARS STOP HERE' and, beneath in white letters on a blue background, 'QUEUE HERE FOR CARS TO CITY'. The advertisements for the *Belfast Telegraph* and Christie's Paints are for local companies still very much in business at the time of writing. *John H. Meredith*

Left Chamberlain 348 waits on the terminal passing loop at Glengormley in January 1949. Although the trolleybus wires have been erected, the trolleybus terminus is a few yards short of the tram terminus and is out of shot behind the camera nearer the city.

The sponsors of the advertisement on the side of the tram proclaiming 'Crosse & Blackwell - Soups that Nourish' are still around and the general disposition of the buildings has changed very little - even the scalloped edges to the barge-boards have been retained by the Cornerstone Estate Agency which now occupies what was then new premises for John Davidson & Co. The 1930s-style telephone kiosk has, however, long since disappeared. *D. G. Coakham*

Centre left The same area today (minus 348, regretfully!) shows that the old telephone box has been replace with a modern BT glass kiosk and the row of houses are almost all shops. The garage in the distance has lost its quaint little tower and is now a thoroughly modern Shell self-service filling station. The modern corrugated structure on the extreme left in front of the Cornerstone Estate Agency is an enclosed public toilet. *Mike Maybin*

Below left Chamberlains 354 and 365 stand in the same position at Glengormley terminus towards the last day of tramcar operation in January 1949. Although the track is double at the terminus, they come together as a single line towards the camera; the reason is that the last half mile or so of the Glengormley route was single track with passing loops, of which this was the final one. The overhead, however, was double all the way. The plate below the 'STOP' sign reads 'QUEUE HERE FOR CARS TO CITY'.

The trolleybus wires are in situ for the commencement of operation on 24 January. Although some of the early turning arrangements at trolleybus termini were reversing triangles, they were converted to turning circles as soon as possible. The only exception was Glengormley, which remained a triangle until closure in 1966. Trolleybuses turned right here into a private road just south of the crossroads, stopped to allow passengers to alight, turned left into a cul-de-sac, reversed around a right-hand turn into another cul-de-sac, then pulled forward to the boarding stop. Passengers were not normally allowed to remain on the trolleybus while reversing. As both sets of frogs were sprung, the manoeuvre was carried out relatively quickly. *D. G. Coakham*

BELFAST TRAMS SINCE 1945

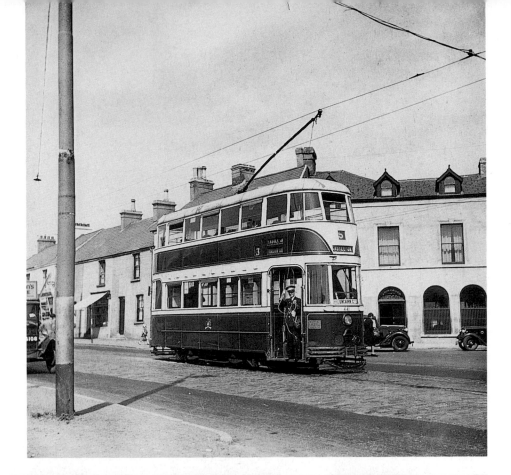

Right Although it was not realised at the time, McCreary 441 was to be the last tram built for use in Belfast - unless we get a Metro like Manchester, a DART like Dublin or a Supertram like Sheffield! This view, again looking out-of-town, was taken at Glengormley terminus in 1947 as the tram was about to return to Castle Junction. Despite the liberal display of destination and route information on roller blinds in front, at the rear and on both sides, some McCrearys and Chamberlains carried 'via' boards at the front on the Glengormley service. This car is for Castle Junction via Duncairn Gardens despite the number 3 in the side route box. The band around the conductor's cap denoted long service. *A. R. Spencer*

Below The NCR (Northern Counties Railway) - sometimes referred to as the LMS (London, Midland & Scottish) or Midland station after its pre-1948 owners who operated it under their Northern Counties Committee (NCC) - had, like the BCDR station, a tram bay, and Moffett 332 is seen here in it having sustained rather a bash to its dash. The posters in the background advertise excursions offered by the newly created British Railways. 332 is, unusually for the period - around 1950 - fully lined out, and apart from the dash panel looks well. The entire station building, magnificent in its heyday, is regrettably no longer there. *John Edgington*

'Rebuild' 164 poses on Shore Road on 25 May 1952. Although the trolleybuses have taken over the all-day service on the Greencastle route - one can just be seen on the extreme left of the picture - trams still operated to Fortwilliam, as the Shore Road Depot was still open when this photograph was taken.

Bus GZ 906 (GZ 3262) is an ex-NIRTB Leyland PS1, which entered service in 1946 with a 53-seater low-bridge Park Royal body, and is seen here in the livery of the Ulster Transport Authority on the Belfast-Carrickfergus-Whitehead route. *H. M. Rea*

This 'full-frontal' view of McCreary 394 outside Shore Road Depot was probably taken in the very early 1950s. The track layout was rather restrictive. There were two trailing curves from the out-of-town track, each of which led to a three-way point, making six tracks in all. Just beyond the depot tracks was a trailing crossover. Trams going to the depot from the City Centre went beyond the depot curve and reversed in, while those from the Greencastle direction needed to reverse over the crossover to gain the out-of-town track, then reverse again into the depot. Cars from the depot to Greencastle could go straight out into service, while those bound for the City Centre direction went out to the 'main line', reversed over the crossover, then on into town. The 'prefabs' on the right have all since been replaced with permanent housing - although only fairly recently. *John Kennedy*

Right Open-topper 244 poses outside Shore Road Depot, having been fitted up as a snow plough. Given that the trolley-bus wires are in position and that the tram wires are tied off just beyond the depot, the date of the photograph is probably 1952. Immediately to the left of 244 is a Belfast Corporation 'CARS STOP BY REQUEST' sign, while in the background between the tram and the canvas-covered van is an Ulster Transport Authority 'BUS STOP' sign. The former sign has black letters on a white ground for the word 'STOP', and a blue border with white letters, while the UTA sign has white letters on a green background.

The houses on the left-hand side of Shore Road are still there, though the gas lights have been replaced by something rather more modern. The name 'Shore Road', incidentally, indicated its proximity to the shore of Belfast Lough, but in recent years the construction of the ten-lane Foreshore Motorway - the M2/M5 - has resulted in Shore Road becoming somewhat more inland! *H. C. Casserley*

Right Another view of 244 taken at the same time from the opposite direction, looking towards the City Centre. The track layout is clearly seen, and the 'sprung' points of the crossover and the depot tracks made the manoeuvres in and out of the depot a little easier.

Although the depot building is now bricked up it is still standing, complete with weather-vane. There is now a block of multi-storey flats in the middle background and the single-storey buildings on the right have been replaced by a row of two-storey shops. *H. B. Priestley*

Left Taken on a foggy January day in 1950, this photograph shows Moffett 299 having its trolley turned at Greencastle terminus preparatory to travelling to Botanic Park (a short working of the Malone Road route).

The newly erected trolleybus wires can just be seen, but it was to be another ten months before the route was converted to trolleybus operation.

This area is completely changed today, and there is a major motorway junction at this point. *John H. Meredith*

IN AND AROUND THE DEPOTS

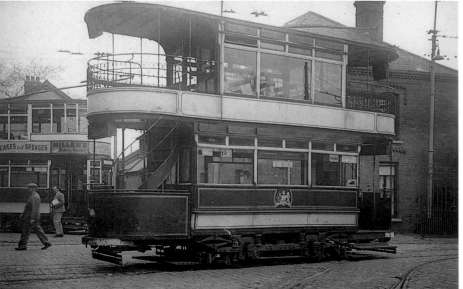

BY 1945 the six depots in use were Knock, Mountpottinger, Sandy Row, Ardoyne, Antrim Road (Salisbury Avenue) and Shore Road; only Falls had been converted to trolleybus operation. Lisburn Road - one of the early horse tram depots - never made the transition to electric traction and neither of the sheds used by the Cavehill & Whitewell Tramway Company was taken over by the Corporation.

Left Standard Red 63 was photographed entering Knock Depot on 9 May 1947. This car acquired roof-mounted route number boxes in the 1920s, and a hangover from the War years was the white-painted bumper bar. The depot track was well worn by this stage.

The photograph was taken just before the depot was closed for operation. Unlike Ardoyne, Falls and Mountpottinger, Knock was never an operational depot for trolley or motor buses, although it was used for storage purposes for some years before being handed over to the Electricity Department. A fair measure of track, including some three-way points, remained in situ until acquired by the Ulster Folk and Transport Museum, which intends to recreate a street scene, the better to display the Belfast trams in their 'natural habitat'. *D. G. Coakham*

Below left A side view of ex-horse car 238 in Knock Depot around 1946. The origins of the ex-horse cars are not absolutely clear, but it is believed that 50 of the best were converted to electric traction in 1905, although to a Manchester design favoured by A. A. Blackburn, the Car Works Superintendent. They were numbered in the series 201-250, the numbers 171-200 being left vacant for future additions to the fleet. At some point - probably before 1910 - they were rebuilt to look like shortened versions of the Standard Reds and probably received top covers at the same time. The wrought iron gate at the front nearside was retained for a period, although 238 had lost its by the time this photograph was taken.

There were several features distinguishing the ex-horse cars from Standard Reds. One of these was that the former had six opening wooden ventilators above the windows in the lower saloon, while the Standards did not. On horse cars the waist panels were significantly deeper than the rocker panels, while on Standard Reds the two panels were about the same depth. The horse cars were also shorter and obviously carried fewer passengers. *R. C. Ludgate*

Right This photograph of Standard Red 141 was taken by John Meredith in June 1948 and shows to good effect the narrow entrance to Mountpottinger Depot, sandwiched between McCracken's shop carrying the poster for Goya perfume and the Picturedrome cinema. The conductor is holding the trolley rope ready to guide the trolley over the complex of facing frogs (overhead points) in the depot proper. The approaching trolleybus is on the Castlereagh route, and the photographer is standing with his back to the terminus. *John H. Meredith*

Left This view, taken on 6 June 1953 on the occasion of the LRTL tour of Belfast tramways, shows the forecourt of Mountpottinger Depot shortly before its closure as an operational tram depot to prepare it for conversion to bus operation. 'Rebuild' 31 is clearly posed here showing the destination 'WATERWORKS ANTRIM ROAD' and route number 69; this rather unusual 'half-moon' style of lettering sometimes used for two-line displays in tram days refers to a route closed in 1949. The detailed lining out and decorative corners on the dash, which 31 carried to the end of its days, can also be seen clearly, as can the depot cat in the right background! The entire depot area has now been redeveloped as a housing estate. *R. J. S. Wiseman*

Right This relatively close-up view of 78 in the depot forecourt at Mountpottinger was also taken in 1953, and just shows a reflection of McCreary 400 in the windows of the lower saloon. Unlike the majority of the 'Rebuild' Class, 78 had top-deck panels the same height all the way round, and looks much the better for it.

Although it is almost impossible to see it in this view, there was a track curving off to the right into Madrid Street yard, close to where the man and children are standing. Initially used as an open-air store, Madrid Street was latterly where retired cars were scrapped (see page 91 and the map on page 36). *John Price*

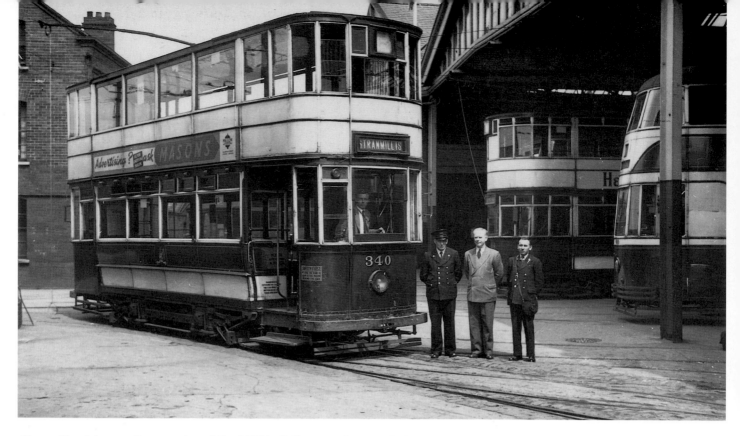

Above Also taken on the occasion of the LRTL's Belfast tour in June 1953, this photograph shows Moffett 340, one of the tour cars, posed just inside the depot gates. The destination 'STRAN-MILLIS' was probably wound up for the photograph, for by this date that route had been converted to bus operation. The two men in 'civilian' dress are members of the tour party; one is R. J. S. Wiseman.

The Union flag can just be discerned flying from the depot manager's upstairs bedroom window and from the flagpole in front of the depot itself. No doubt this was in honour of the recent **Coronation.** *Courtesy David Harvey*

Below It was very difficult to get a good picture of the depot fan at Mountpottinger because of the exceptionally narrow entrance. Initially this entrance was laid with double track, but when the track was lifted in Mountpottinger Road between Bridge End and the depot at the beginning of the war, the entrance layout was reduced to a single track from the upper Mountpottinger Road. This view shows clearly the track disappearing off to the left into Madrid Street yard, initially used as for permanent way storage, but latterly used for scrapping tramcars. The precise date of this photograph is not known, but judging form the proliferation of flags and apparently well-dressed and enthusiastic visitors, it is possibly again June 1953. *C. Carter*

Right Belfast City Tramways had two water cars, A and B, and A is seen here returning to Mountpottinger Depot. Before the days of full-width road paving and with the dust created by drying horse droppings, it was necessary to spray the roadways frequently in an attempt to keep the dust down as much as possible. The water car was delivered in 1905, remained in service until 1932 and was painted brown. *Photographer unknown*

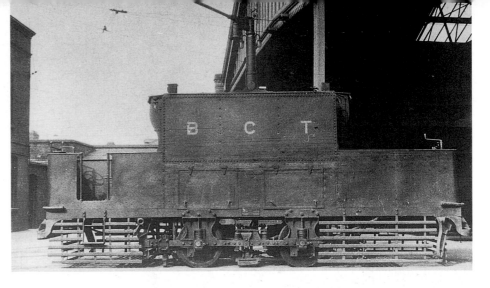

Below This photograph of Madrid Street Yard was taken shortly after the trams were abandoned and shows part of the process of breaking them up. Cars were driven in small groups into the yard beside Mountpottinger Depot (the entrance tracks to which were beyond the gates in the background), prior to having the top decks removed with the help of the mobile crane in the picture. Metal parts suitable for scrap were recovered, often by cutting, and the wooden parts of the bodies were burned. Chamberlains 365 and 382 are seen here receiving 'the treatment'.

The large white-painted brick building in the background is the thousand-seater Picturedrome cinema, itself to be demolished shortly after Mountpottinger Depot closed in the 1970s. *Belfast Telegraph*

Above Chamberlain 382 stands in Sandy Row about to take up duty, although the destination screen does not give much help in suggesting whither it might be bound! The track layout at Sandy Row Depot approach was complex (see the map on page 55). There were double junctions with the Lisburn Road in both directions, which almost immediately converged into a single track in Sandy Row itself. Single tracks then led into Napier Street to the works, paint shop and former tram-body-building area, and into Gaffikin Street leading into the depot fan of 20 (later 19) roads. Both Napier Street and Gaffikin Street had long double-track passing places.

Although heavily rebuilt, Sandy Row itself is still clearly recognisable. *H. B. Priestley*

Below A view of stores van No 8 in Napier Street, posed on the passing loop to allow the McCreary to go into the works. Like Ardoyne Depot there was an entrance arch with a clock, but the narrowness of the access made it very difficult to appreciate the design of the depot. Today absolutely nothing remains of the depot, houses or street layout. *H. B. Priestley*

Seen inside the redeveloped Sandy Row works, Nos 2 and 3 among others are just being prepared for service shortly after electrification. A disused horse car is in the background on the right of the picture. The track layout is very complicated in order to allow cars to be shunted around with as little disturbance as possible to others. *Green Collection, Ulster Folk and Transport Museum*

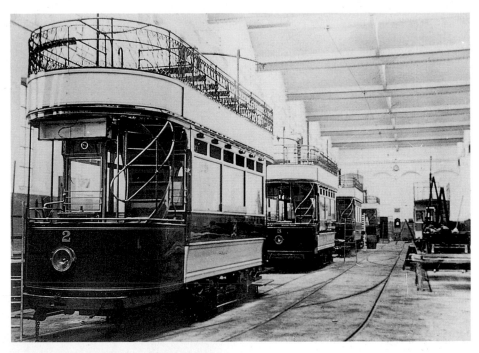

Probably taken some time in the early 1950s, this view shows another part of Sandy Row works where the overhead crane is capable of lifting the body from its truck preparatory to major overhaul or repair. *C. Wilson*

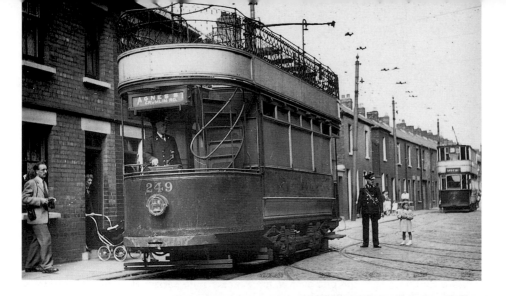

Left Brought out into Gaffikin Street specially for the occasion of the LRTL tour of June 1953 is 249 with her windows so dirty that they appear to have been painted out, having been relegated to purely works duties for some years. The storage tracks into the depot (there were originally 20, later reduced to 19) can clearly be seen to the right of this picture, looking towards Sandy Row, as can Moffett 340, which was the tram used for the actual tour. *R. J. S. Wiseman*

Below left Now we can see the opposite side of Gaffikin Street as the June sunshine casts something of a shadow over part of the Sandy Row depot. According to *Tramway and Railway World* of 12 October 1905 the depot could hold a maximum of 69 cars. The trackwork was complicated and exacting, with all the curves being transitional and true to within one-sixteenth of an inch (1.5 mm). Nevertheless the cars worked in and out very well, although one old hand was quoted as saying that another coat of paint would have made the trams too wide for the narrow entrances!

Although not discernible in this picture, there was a passing place further down Gaffikin Street. Although trams came to within about 3 or 4 feet of the front door of a number of houses, there were surprisingly few accidents. Perhaps the fact that many of the residents of the street worked for the Tramways Department served to sharpen their awareness of the trams. *J. G. Gillham*

Right McCreary 414 was photographed after a collision with an empty coal train at the junction of Old Channel Road and Queen's Road on 13 November 1950. As the tramcar was on its way to pick up workers from the shipyard it was empty at the time, and there were no casualties. It is seen here in Gaffikin Street while parked briefly in Sandy Row depot. It was later transferred to Shore Road Depot until a decision was made regarding repair. In the event it was used for spare parts. *Courtesy Deputy Keeper, Public Record Office for Northern Ireland*

Right 'Rebuild' 159 and Moffett 319 are seen here on the approach tracks to Ardoyne Depot, leaving and entering service, around the same time that the photograph on page 73 was taken in August 1952, as Kerr's lorry is again in evidence. 159, showing the incorrect destination 'CASTLE JN.', is waiting until 319 clears the single track outside the depot (see the map on page 66). By this time some cars worked to the crossover at Marlborough Park on the Lisburn Road rather than to the 'regular' short working at Windsor Grounds. The lack of route number displays suggests that both cars were on non-timetabled journeys.

The waste ground to the left was shortly made into a bus turning circle, while the land behind and to the left of the depot was developed into a bus garage that remained in service until 1993. The lorry carries a Northern Ireland goods vehicle licence plate near the bottom of the door. *Roy Brook*

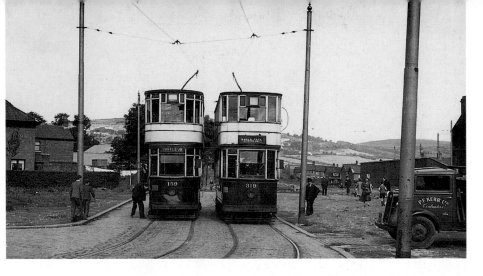

Below left 'Rebuild' 275 leaves Ardoyne Depot in June 1953. Although tucked away in a suburb of North Belfast, the design of the depot entrance arch surmounted by a handsome clock was quite impressive. Opened in 1913, it was one of the larger depots, capable of holding 84 cars. It also held the distinction of being the last tram depot to close. From the entrance track 12 tracks led to

the pits over which the cars were parked at night. *Courtesy David Harvey*

Below right Taken a few months before the trams were abandoned, this view of the inside of Ardoyne Depot demonstrates the track-layer's art well. The depot fan, comprised of transitional curves and complex crossings, led to the storage roads. A short siding outside the depot can just be seen at the foot of the picture. I don't believe that it was used very often, but it would have been useful in depot shunting or when two cars met on the single-line depot approach. *J. C. Gillham*

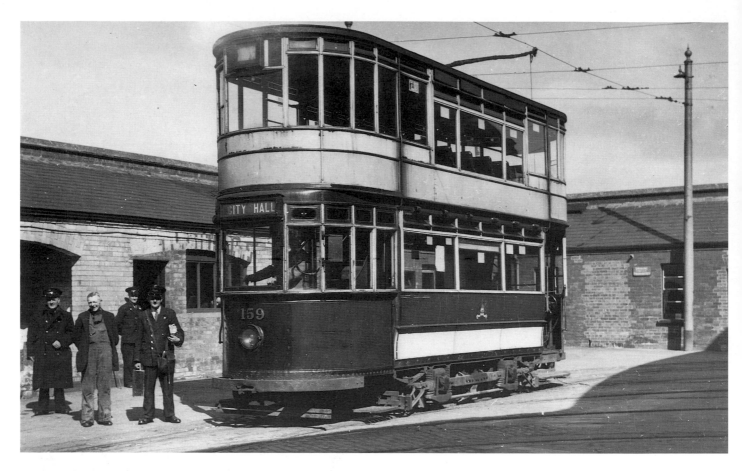

Above This view of 'Rebuild' 159 was taken in Ardoyne Depot in June 1953. The conductor is carrying one of the then new Ultimate ticket machines, which greatly speeded up the task of issuing tickets and in addition maintained a count of the number of tickets sold at nine different fares. This information, in conjunction with conductors' waybills, helped the Traffic Department to analyse passenger travel patterns, from which future requirements might be deduced. These statistics were also used to monitor the effects of changes to fares and stages. *Courtesy David Harvey*

Below Taken in April 1954, about two months after the trams were abandoned, Chamberlains 353, 349 and 360 rest in Ardoyne Depot before being driven to Madrid Street Yard for scrapping. Each of the trams was advertising the (then) new CinemaScope at the Royal Hippodrome. The Last Tram Procession on 28 February 1954, in which each of these trams took part, resulted in souvenir hunters carrying away bells, light bulbs, destination blinds and anything else portable. 349 is missing its front destination and route number blind, while 356 has just lost the route number blind. *Cliff Brown*

Chamberlain 368 is seen here heading along Salisbury Avenue towards Antrim Road Depot, which was located in that road off the Antrim Road just south of Fortwilliam Park. Salisbury Avenue was a small depot and catered mainly for the cars operating the Glengormley services (see the map on page 81). The entrance to it was very awkward and cars bound for the depot from the city stopped just past the entrance to Salisbury Avenue, reversed into the road then reversed again into the depot. Cars from Glengormley passed the road junction and reversed into the depot 'wrong road' along Salisbury Avenue itself. Cars from the depot reversed this procedure, again travelling 'wrong road' when necessary. Although in today's terms this process sounds very hazardous from a traffic point of view, there was very little motor traffic in the late 1940s and Salisbury Avenue was, and is, a relatively quiet residential street. Collisions were rare. *D. G. Coakham*

Like the majority of tram depots in Belfast, access to Shore Road was very tight and this view of Moffett 298 illustrates the point well. Though the photograph is not dated, I would estimate that it would be about 1951 or 1952. *R. C. Jackson*

PRESERVED CARS AND TICKETS

THERE is no valid reason for lumping these two categories together in the one section other than the fact that there only four photographs between them!

Below Ex-horse tram 249 was photographed in the temporary premises in a former engine shed near Queen's Quay in September 1955 after first-class restoration by the Corporation

Transport Department. The former Belfast Corporation was fortunately sufficiently far-sighted to procure and preserve a number of important transport items and exhibited them for a short time in premises besides Queen's Quay station. The collection was later expanded and moved to larger premises at nearby Witham Street.

At the re-organisation of local government in 1973 the collection was merged with the new Ulster Folk and Transport Museum. Although the UFTM's headquarters were in Cultra, the transport exhibits remained in Belfast for many years. A new gallery has recently opened on the Cultra site specifically to display large railway items and there is a public commitment by the Museum's Director to display the trams and other 'road' items as soon as the premises currently under construction are completed. *F. Kelso*

Below left There is some doubt whether this photograph legitimately can be included in a book purporting to look at Belfast's trams since 1945, but John Price, who kindly donated it, made a very persuasive case for doing so!

Horse car 118 is seen in the former paint shop of Sandy Row Depot in 1963, having been beautifully restored by the Transport Department to its 1905 condition in preparation for the Lord Mayor's Show of that year. Following its appearance in the procession it was placed in the Transport Museum in Witham Street, and remained there until the Museum's closure. It is now due to be transferred to the new Road Gallery at the UFTM's Cultra site when it opens in 1995 or 1996.

Unfortunately very few details have survived about individual trams in the horse car fleet, so the following comments inevitably contain an element of speculation. 118 was probably bought new in about 1897. A photograph of 119, taken in about 1900, shows a seven-window car, and 118 may originally have been similar. During the period 1902-3 the entire fleet was altered to three-window layout and fitted with more modern 'Lincrusta' ceilings, and this picture of 118 shows the result.

The 'BST Co' monogram was used in the early 1890s, but photographic evidence suggests that its use had died out by the end of the century. However, the legend 'BELFAST CITY TRAMWAYS' was added to the rocker panels from 1 January 1905. Belfast is believed to have been the first city to adopt roller blind destination boxes, and this one was operated simply by turning a knob at the end of each roller. The lettering was black on a white cloth background, although this was reversed when electric cars took over. The legend 'THE LIFEBOAT RULE IS WOMEN AND CHILDREN FIRST' began to be added from about 1900.

One gets the impression from contemporary photographs that perhaps the dash is rather 'flatter' on the restored car than on the original. However, the car has remained in very good condition during the last 30 years, and although some of the parts are made of modern materials, 118 is probably one of the best preserved horse trams in the United Kingdom. *David Irwin*

Opposite page above Chamberlain 357 was also photographed at Queen's Quay. Although out on the last day of 'normal' operation, 357 did not take part in the official Last Tram Procession, and therefore did not suffer the same fate as some that had various items removed by souvenir-hunters.

With preservation in mind, 357 was transferred from Ardoyne to Mountpottinger Depot on 16 June 1954 and beautifully restored by Transport Department staff before being displayed in the former rail-motor shed near Queen's Quay.

On 1 April 1962 the new Transport Museum in Witham Street opened, and 357, along with other Belfast trams, was put on public display. The Museum, run by the then Belfast Corporation, took the unusual and enlightened step (for 1962) of allowing public access to a number of steam engines as well as trams 249 and 357. It is not surprising that the trams subsequently became part of a children's adventure playground for a relatively deprived area of East Belfast. What is surprising is the remarkably good condition both vehicles are still in, after 30 years of such freedom!

357 is currently in storage pending the opening of the purpose-built premises at the UFTM's Cultra site. *Dennis Gill*

Below right This selection of tickets illustrates the range used after the War.

All the tickets on the top row and the first three from the left on the bottom are known as 'Bell Punch' tickets. Under this system the conductor issued the appropriate value ticket and punched a hole in the relevant place to denote an inward, outward or cross-town journey. There were other markings, 'A', 'B' and sometimes 'W', on some tickets, but these were not used regularly.

The first two pairs of tickets, VL 412 0001/EG 466 9854 and GP 422 8888/QH 607 8841, are 1d white and 2d orange respectively, and were used during the 1930s. They are labelled 'BELFAST CITY TRAMWAYS' and the 1d ticket could be punched for a cross-town journey if required. The 'fine print' on 8888 reads 'This ticket is issued subject to the Bye-laws and should be retained by the passenger and, when used for transfer, handed to the Omnibus Conductor'. Additionally there was the facility to punch for transfer between tram and bus.

The next four tickets, QF 17 4005, XQ 72 1564, BL 17 7600 and DC 8 1792 were 1/2d blue, 1d white, 2d purple, and 3d green respectively. The 1d and 3d were issued in 1940 - the dates of the issue of the others are unknown. To increase the range of discrete serial numbers, each depot issued its own tickets with unique code letters. These appeared on the top left hand of the tickets, just about where the serial letters were previously, and the serial letters moved up to the top right-hand corner. Thus the 1d ticket was issued by Mountpottinger depot (MP), the 2d by Antrim Road (AN), and the 3d by Knock (K). (The 1/2d was issued by Haymarket trolleybus depot in East Belfast - I do not have a 1/2d tram ticket - sorry about that!) The other codes were AR (Ardoyne), SR (Sandy Row) and SH (Shore Road); P was for petrol buses based at Falls Road. The 'fine print' and transfer facility are identical to QP 422 8888. This system increased the theoretical availability of numbers considerably, and given that the Undertaking carried well over 200 million passengers annually in the years after the war, the need for additional space can easily be appreciated.

The final group of tickets, DA 15765/6 and GA 04968, were known as 'Ultimates' from the name of the ticket machine that issued them. The tickets were headed 'BELFAST CORPN TRANSPORT DEPT', and the 'fine print' reads 'Issued subject to Bye-laws and Regs. Not Transferable'. The issuing machine printed the stage number at which the passenger boarded. Odd numbers denoted outward journeys from the City Centre, beginning with '01', while even numbers were used for inward journeys, beginning with '02' at the most distant terminus (Glengormley at that time). 18 was used for the stage immediately before the City Centre, while Stage 20 was reserved for cross-town journeys. The stage number could be printed in one of three locations.

Depending on the value of the ticket, up to three of the following designations could be used: 'ORD', 'W'PEOPLE', 'CHILD' and 'X-TOWN'. However, the machine could not count the numbers of tickets issued at different stages; this information was recorded by the conductor on his waybill. *Mike Maybin*

This index includes both streets and well-known Belfast landmarks featured in the photographs.